About the Author

Huw Barker Rahane took a degree in business studies in South Africa, travelled widely before settling down to a career in journalism and public relations. He retired to devote himself to writing. He now lives in Sussex.

To my Wife, the Well-Beloved

Portrait of Thomas Hardy by Augustus Edwin John, 1923

Huw Barker Rahane

WHO'S WHO IN THOMAS HARDY

AN INDEX OF THE CHARACTERS IN HARDY'S MAJOR PROSE FICTION

AUSTIN MACAULEY
PUBLISHERS LTD.

A CIP catalogue record for this title is available from the British Library.

ISBN 978 178455 020 2

www.austinmacauley.com

First Published (2014)
Austin Macauley Publishers Ltd.
25 Canada Square
Canary Wharf
London
E14 5LB

Printed and bound in Great Britain

Contents

HUW BARKER RAHANE

Hardy's work often seems lost in a sea of comment and analysis. This survey seeks to go past all this into the clear water of listing the men and woman who people the pages of his major fiction, without exegesis, value judgements or location guides; just a list of those who *materially* advance or illustrate the plot. The purpose is to be useful to anyone wishing to find out quickly who Marty South loved in vain or who shot Sergeant Troy.

It is my hope that by making plain facts easily available it will stimulate interest in the genius of Thomas Hardy and promote pleasure in the quite enormous sea of riches that lie forgotten or unrecognised behind the few over-exposed and sometimes over-praised parts of this *oeuvre*.

H.B.R.
Sussex 2014

The Key

The novels	Code	Characters
Desperate Remedies	DR	11
Far from the Madding Crowd	FMC	6
Hand of Ethelberta, The	HE	13
Jude the Obscure	JO	11
Laodicean, A	Al	13
Mayor of Casterbridge, The	MC	8
Pair of Blue Eyes, A	PBE	15
Return of the Native, The	RN	7
Tess of the D'Urbervilles	TESS	8
Trumpet-Major, The	TM	10
Two on a Tower	TT	5
Under the Greenwood Tree	UGT	7
Well-Beloved, The	WB	8
Woodlanders, The	WOOD	8

The collections	Code	Characters
A Changed Man and Other Tales	CM	21
A Group of Noble Dames	GND	18
Life's Little Ironies	LL	30
Wessex Tales	WT	11
Total of listed characters		**210**

The Register

Name   **Book**

A number after the code indicates the number of the work within a collection

Aldclyffe, Miss, proud landowner	DR
Alicia, diarist	CM (3)
Aspent, Car'line, entranced teenager	LL (7)
Barnet, George	WT (5)
Baxby, Lady Anna, a suspicion unfounded	GND (7)
Bell, Barbara, grasping actress	Al
Benbow, Marcia, Jocelyn's new beloved	WB
Boldwood. William, good but glum	FMC
Bridehead, Sue, Jude's beloved	JO
Brook, Rhoda, laid a spell	WT (4)
Caroline, Marchioness of Stonehenge	GND (3)
Cannister, Martin, sexton	PBE
Caro, Avice, the first great love	WB
Caro, Ann Avice, the second great love	WB
Caro, Avice, the third great love	WB
Cartlett, pub landlord	JO26
Charmond, Felice, femme fatale	WOOD
Chickerel, Picotee, Ethelberta's sister	HE
Chickerel, R, Ethelberta's father	HE

Dorrell, Thomas, Betty's father	CM (2)
D'Urberville, Alec, seducer	TESS
D'Urberville, Mrs, Alec's mother	TESS
Durbeyfield, John, Tess's father	TESS
Durbeyfield, Joan, Tess's mother	TESS
Durbeyfield, Tess, luckless milkmaid	TESS
Edlin, Mrs, Drusilla's friend	JO
Everard, Christine, country maiden	CM (2)
Everard, squire	CM (2)
Everdene, Bathsheba, enduring heroine	FMC
Farfrae, Donald, conquering Scot	MC
Father Time, Jude's son	JO
Fawley, Drusilla, Jude's aunt	JO
Fawley, Jude, idealistic stonemason	JO
Fitzpiers, Dr Edred, priapic medic	WOOD
Frankland, Frances	LL (3)
Frankland Mrs Leonora, music teacher	LL (3)
Garland, Anne, loved by two brothers	TM
Garland, Martha, Anne's mother	TM
George, King of England	TM
Gillingham, George, schoolteacher	JO
Glanville, Louis	TT
Goodman, Mrs., Paula Power's chaperone	AL
Graye, Ambrose, architect of long ago	DR
Graye, Cytherea, with sapphire-blue eyes	DR

Graye, Owen, architect	DR
Grebe, Barbara, cruelly-treated wife	GND (2)
Grebe, Sir John, Barbara's father	GND (2)
Grove, Phyllis, loses two suitors	WT (3)
Haddegan, David, devious businessman	CM (11)
Halborough, Cornelius, gentle curate	LL (4)
Halborough, Joshua, tougher curate	LL (4)
Hall, Sally	WT (6)
Hampstonshire, Duchess of, pursued her love	GND (9)
Hanning, Emily, shy and delicate	LL (6)
Hardcome, James, swaps betrothed	LL (8b)
Hardcome, Steve, swaps betrothed	LL (8b)
Hardy, Captain, HMS Victory	TM
Harnham, Mrs Edith, gentle employer	LL (5)
Havill, bogus architect	AL
Heymere, Maria, twice-married beauty	GND (5)
Haze, Cunningham, police chief	AL
Helmsdale, Cuthbert, stand-in father	TT
Henchard,Michael, the Mayor	MC
Henchard, Susan, naïve wife	MC
Higham, Theophilus, curate	CM (3)
Hinton, Adelaide, secret fiancée	DR
Hipcroft, Ned, discarded suitor	LL (7)
Hobson, Sam, loyal gardener	LL (2)
Holway, Luke, soldier	CM (4)

Petrick, Squire, snobbish landowner	GND (6)
Phelpson, Charley, changed his mind	GND (1)
Phillotson, Richard, schoolmaster	JO
Phippard, Joanna, gets her man	LL (6)
Pierston, Isaac, marries Anne Avice Caro	WB
Pierston, Jocelyn, man who loves well	WB
Pine-Avon, Nicola, widow	WB
Power, Abner, anarchist and plotter	AL
Power, Paula, heiress	AL
Privett, William, haunting figure	LL (8c)
Puddingcome, Nicholas, band leader	LL (8f)
Raunham, Rev. Mr, local rector	DR
Raye, Charles, barrister	LL (5)
Reynard, Stephen, man who keeps faith	GND (1)
Robin, Fanny, cast aside	FMC
Sargent, Netty, saves her home	LL (8i)
Satchel, Andrey, tipsy groom	LL (8d)
Satchel, Andrey Senior, bogus fiddler	LL (8e)
Savile, Lucy	WT (5)
Seaway, Anne, stand-in wife	DR
Shinar, Fred, no-hope swain	UGT
Smallbury, Lydia (Liddy)	FMC
Smith, Mrs Jane, Stephen's mother	PBE
Smith, John, Stephen's father	PBE
Smith, Stephen, Elfride's first suitor	PBE

Uplandtowers, Earl of, stern husband	GND (2)
Vannicock, Lieut. soldier-actor	CM (1)
V--, Mademoiselle	CM (8)
Venn, Diggory, the man in red	RN
Vilbert, 'Physician', pill-peddling charlatan	JO
Vye, Eustacia, heathland Lorelei	RN
Whittle, Abel, late for work	MC
Wildeve, Damon, mesmerised by love	RN
Willowes, Edmond, scarred lover	GND (2)
Winter, Jack, tragic thief	LL (8g)
Winterborne, Giles, deeply loved	WOOD
Woodwell, Rev., nonconformist preacher	AL
Worm, William, Swancourt's manservant	PBE
Yeobright, Clym, returning native	RN
Yeobright, Mrs, unhappy mother	RN
Yeobright, Thomasin, married wrong man	RN

Total of listed characters   **210**

Part I: The Novels

DESPERATE REMEDIES

Pretty Cytherea Graye is wooed by architect Edward Spingrove and has a job with rich Miss Aldclyffe, who wants her to marry her steward, the handsome Manston; on the night they are married, was it Manston's first wife who was spotted alive, in which case there is dirty work? A chase ensues, Cytherea's honour is saved, Miss Aldclyffe turns out to be Manston's mother; Manston turns out to have murdered his wife; Cytherea marries Spingrove.

*****ALDCLYFFE, MISS,** 46, tall, majestic, impetuous, is owner of a 1,000-acre estate; she gives young Cytherea Graye a job, and shows her a locket with a picture Cytherea recognises as her father, Miss Aldclyffe tells her sadly of a lost love.

Miss Aldclyffe appoints Manston as her estate steward despite her lawyer's strong advice that he is a dubious character.

The original Cytherea Bradleigh was in her youth betrayed and had a love-child, Aeneas Manston; she changed her name to Aldclyffe – that is why she insisted on Manston as her steward; she sees Cytherea as the ideal wife for her son.

CHINNEY, JOSEPH, railway porter, gives evidence at inquest of Mrs Eunice Manston that he took her to the Three Tranters Inn where there was a fire; on the night of the wedding of Manston and Cytherea, Chinney reveals he saw a strange woman (Mrs Manston?) take the train back to London; this sparks a chase to intercept the newlyweds.

GRAYE, AMBROSE, before the story begins, falls in love with Cytherea Bradleigh but they are parted by circumstances; he marries someone else and has a son Owen and a daughter he names Cytherea after the early love he never forgot and who had changed her name to … Aldclyffe.

***GRAYE, CYTHEREA,** 18, has 'magnificent resources in face and bosom', with graceful, sapphire-blue eyes and a fine head of hair; she sees her father Ambrose killed on a building site; she and her brother Owen are left poor and seek a new life in another town to make a living; she meets Owen's colleague Edward Spingrove; she and Edward go boating, they declare their love but she cools off when he says there is something he has hidden from her (it is Adelaide Hinton) but he does not explain.

On the first night of attending to Miss Aldclyffe, she is shown a locket; when the employer opens it, C. recognises the picture is of her father; some hours later Miss Aldclyffe enters C's room, gets into bed with her, kisses her passionately and urges: 'don't let any man stand between us'; she urges C. to say her prayers as usual and hears her pray for her brother Owen and for her swain Edward Spingrove; she comments that Edward is a worthless young man who already has a fiancée.

Next day C. learns about Edward's earlier love Hinton and writes to end the relationship; she meets Manston and they are much drawn to each other; later, after the reported death of Eunice Manston there is pressure all around her to accept him; on Old Christmas Eve (Jan 5) things happen – she marries Manston, Spingrove learns he has been jilted by Hinton, and it transpires a Mrs Manston secretly left the inn for London just before fire at the inn.

As C.'s marriage is now apparently illegal there is a chase to stop the honeymoon trip going ahead; Owen catches up with his sister and brings her to his own place; Edward declares his love again, marries Cytherea.

GRAYE, OWEN, architect like his father Ambrose, introduces his sister to colleague Springrove; there is a crisis when

Owen's health and finances deteriorate and Miss Aldclyffe promises to look after him if his sister marries Manston, so he presses Cytherea; finally his health and finances recover.

HINTON, ADELAIDE, 29, jilts Spingrove and marries rich elderly farmer Bollens.

*****MANSTON, AENEAS,** appointed land steward to Miss Aldclyffe's estate following her manipulation of the selection process; Manston meets Cytherea who is struck by his elegant manners, ruby lips and face of delicate beauty; he tells her he is troubled but does not say by what; he falls in love with her before Miss Aldclyffe orders him to take his wife back; after he is free he is direct in his pressure on Cytherea and she refuses to marry him; the pressure mounts as he says he is willing to have Owen live with him; she relents; he marries her, the couple are found just in time to stop the honeymoon journey; Manston, having killed Eunice and being deprived of Cytherea, has to present some kind of wife on the Aldclyffe estate in order to preserve his status and his job; he hunts out for – and finds – a woman of the same height and age to impersonate Eunice called Seaway; after he goes on the run he first makes for Cytherea's house as he is still besotted with her as his legal wife; Edward Spingrove gets there just in time to wrestle him to the ground; later Manston hangs himself in the county gaol.

MANSTON, EUNICE, American actress briefly married to Manston visits him surreptitiously; he kills her.

RAUNHAM, rector at the Aldclyffe estate, hears Chinney's secret and urges the boys to go chase the newlyweds Manston and Cytherea to London; goes to tell Miss Aldclyffe his suspicions about the steward; Raunham notices her 'extraordinary interest in the wellbeing of her steward'; Raunham hires detective who tracks Manston.

SEAWAY, ANNE, needy adventuress; Manston gets her to impersonate Eunice.

*****SPRINGROVE, EDWARD**, architect, about 26, dark hair, intellectual face, meets Owen Graye's sister Cytherea; they go boating together and fall in love, then he writes to her that he is now in an honourable way of freeing himself, but does not explain; Miss Aldclyffe speaks of young Edward as a womaniser; Cytherea ends the relationship when she hears about Miss Hinton; Hinton having thrown Edward over, Cytherea meets him now as a free man and they renew their pledge of love; after she goes to live with Owen following the marriage débâcle he proposes, but she refuses; Edward is outraged about Manston and tells Owen that he suspects the man knew more than he revealed, i.e., his pursuit of Cytherea was plain seduction; Edward starts playing detective in London and finds out about Manston and Seaway; when he next comes to Cytherea's cottage he gets there just in time when 'panting desperado' Manston is trying to abduct her; he wrestles Manston to the floor; finally he marries Cytherea – and takes her boating as he did three years before.

FAR FROM THE MADDING CROWD

*In the deep Dorset outback, three suitors, one girl: Number 3
kills Number 2 – so Number 1 wins the day*

*****BOLDWOOD, WILLIAM,** aged 41, wealthy gentleman-
farmer with extensive land adjoining that of independent
farmer Bathsheba Everdene; under reserved façade burns
intense nature; Bathsheba sends a light-hearted valentine with
message 'Marry Me' which deeply upsets him; he proposes
marriage, making promises for her future ranging from the
grandiose to the pathetic – 'you shall have a pony-carriage of
your own'; she asks that he give her time; when he asks her a
second time, this proud man sinks to his knees but again gets
an evasive answer; when he sees her after she has met Troy he
tells her that his own love is 'strong as death' and that Troy
with his 'unfathomable lies' has stolen his love; he warns her:
'keep him away from me!'; he waylays Troy on his way back
from Bath and tries to buy him off; Troy reveals he is already
married to Bathsheba and contemptuously throws the money
back at him; seething, Boldwood threatens revenge. Boldwood
organises a Christmas Eve party where he extracts from
Bathsheba a pledge about marriage because he believes she is
now a widow. Troy enters, demands that she come back and
Boldwood shoots him dead; Boldwood is gaoled.

*****EVERDENE, BATHSHEBA,** well-favoured, good figure,
in her early twenties, with thick black hair, is an enterprising
free-spirited woman (so cool on a galloping horse she can lie
flat against its back to let low-hanging tree branches pass over
her).
    i) Oak to Boldwood: she meets Gabriel Oak and he soon
proposes marriage; she says she is not ready for that ('I want to
be tamed – I am too independent'); she takes over her uncle's
farm; some months later Oak's presence of mind saves her

property from a huge fire and (as he is now out of work) she gives him a job he asks for – her shepherd; she is haughty at first, then relations become matter-of-fact though he continues to love her; on impulse she sends a valentine to neighbouring farmer Boldwood with the inscription 'Marry Me' which throws him completely; when he asks her three months later to marry him she apologises for what she realises is a joke taken too seriously, and tactfully asks for time.

ii) Boldwood to Troy: when she meet Sergeant Troy the soldier calls her 'Beauty' and she is intrigued; from now on whenever they meet he flatters her and her feeling for him grows; she is overwhelmed when he gives a scintillating display of swordsman's skills for her alone; she is warned against him; she chases after him in Bath where she marries him. Within weeks she is distressed when he drinks and gambles away her money; in Fanny Robin's coffin she also finds a baby's body; she sees Troy kissing Fanny's corpse; Troy rejects her and tells her Fanny was his real love.

iii) Troy to Oak: when her husband has vanished she refuses to believe he is dead; at a Christmas party Boldwood organises he extracts a promise about future marriage, but Troy enters and demands her return; swooning, she screams when he touches her; after Troy is shot dead she tends the body; a year later she is distressed when Oak says he wants to quit; she goes to seek him out and they talk realities; in the end their staff toast 'neighbour Oak and his comely bride'.

***OAK, GABRIEL**, curly-haired warm-hearted shepherd, 28, meets young pretty Bathsheba Everdene and proposes marriage, but she declines; he has bought 200 sheep on credit with the idea of becoming his own man; he leaves them overnight with a badly-trained dog which chases the flock into a chalk-pit; he is ruined and has to start again, offering his services as a shepherd in the local market-place; he goes looking elsewhere and passes a hay-rick on fire with local rustics circling helplessly; he takes charge, mobilises them and prevents the blaze from causing huge damage; a woman on a horse turns up to thank him; it is landowner Bathsheba; she thanks him and he is hired as her shepherd – former suitor is now servant; some time later when she asks him his opinion of the Valentine message to Boldwood and he tells her how wrong she was, she sacks him on the spot, but is forced to take him back immediately when her sheep fall ill and only his country skills save the entire flock; underneath his quiet surface he keeps loving her; he angers her when he warns her again that Troy is not to be trusted; he is in silent despair when he hears of the marriage; remains silently loyal and faithful; a year after Troy's death he feels his love is hopeless and gives notice to quit; Bathsheba rushes to see him, they start to talk about basics, they marry.

*****ROBIN, FANNY**, 19, Bathsheba's former maid, dies in childbirth; Bathsheba, fearing the worst, opens her coffin and finds inside the body of the child she bore Troy; Troy tells Bathsheba he loved Fanny alone and, filled with remorse, orders an expensive (£27) tombstone.

SMALLBURY, LIDDY (Lydia), Bathsheba's petite and faithful companion at the farmhouse; warns her against Troy but Bathsheba says she loves him to distraction; when Fanny Robin's body is brought back Liddy warns Bathsheba a baby will also be found in the coffin; Liddy is witness when Bathsheba marries Oak.

*****TROY, SERGEANT FRANK,** aged 23/24, 11th Dragoon Guards, son of a Parisian woman reputedly by an aristocrat; he reluctantly comes to a church to marry Fanny Robin but she goes to the wrong church, which is a pretext for him not to marry her at all; he meets independent farmer Bathsheba Everdene and sweet-talks her until she is besotted and marries him; when Fanny dies and the body is brought back, he kneels remorsefully and kisses it as his wife watches – Bathsheba is frantic and he tells her that he is a bad black-hearted man but that Fanny is his 'very, very wife'; filled with romantic grief he has an expensive tombstone put over the grave. He decorates it with flowers. He wanders disconsolately to the coast, goes swimming, is swept away by the current, gets picked up by a fishing boat and starts a new life; a year later he is the horseman star of a circus show which visits the country fair which Bathsheba attends but she fails to recognise him in his disguise; he makes a surprise entrance at Boldwood's party and demands she come back to him; as she cringes Boldwood shoots him dead; Troy is buried in Fanny Robin's grave.

THE HAND OF ETHELBERTA

Iron-willed Ethelberta is, at 21, a successful published poet who starts a career giving one-woman shows in London telling stories of her own devising; there is tension in that her public must believe she is upper-crust, not the daughter of a butler (Mr Chickerel); four men pursue her: poet Julian, painter Ladywell, socialite Neigh and the man who finally wins her hand, elderly peer Mountclere.

CHICKEREL, PICOTEE, younger sister of the heroine Ethelberta, is a pupil teacher asked by E. to see that a copy of the volume of poetry she has written gets to her one-time admirer Christopher Julian; Picotee falls for him herself and pines for him; after E. is well settled she marries him.

CHICKEREL, Mr R., Ethelberta's father, butler in mansion where host is surprised when his servant takes an interest in literary matters, not knowing that the poetry his guests are talking about is the work of his butler's daughter (Hardy's social satire); below stairs, Chickerel writes to E. that her verses are being widely praised and advises her to keep her origins secret; time passes, and E. sets him and the family up in a comfortable villa.

CHICKEREL, Mrs, invalid mother to E., Picotee and eight other children: daughters Gwendoline, Georgina. Cornelia, Emmeline, Myrtle, and sons Sol(omon), Dan and Joseph (Joey); many come to help keep house for E.

JULIAN, CHRISTOPHER, West Country music teacher, a slight, thoughtful, over-sensitive young man living with his sister Faith; he meets E. on a country walk and it revives memories of a teenage love; he sets one of her poems to music; declares his love but is rebuffed; when he hears of the coming marriage of E. and Mountclere he joins the unsuccessful chase to stop the wedding, he marries Picotee.

JULIAN, FAITH, Christopher's diffident sister; sees E. perform her show and thinks she is clever – but not very nice.

LADYWELL, still in his early twenties, with eyebrows 'arched high like a girl's', a diffident society painter; falls in love with E.; he hangs in the Royal Academy an idealised picture of E. in Elizabethan garb with an attendant knight, perhaps he himself; one of the three suitors converging on the Rouen hotel where E. has come but he is told to wait, feels he has been deceived.

MENLOVE, Lady Petherwin's flirtatious maid, light-haired and slightly built, finds out for E. where Julian lives; wheedles out of E.'s teenage brother Joey the truth about her family.

MOUNTCLERE, the Hon. EDGAR, leads the chase, with butler Chickerel, his son Sol Chickerel and Julian, to stop E. marrying his brother; they arrive too late.

MOUNTCLERE. Viscount, about 65, jowly, giggly, 'lively old nobleman', much struck by E.'s beauty at a dinner, is told about her background by his footman Tipman who is paid to keep quiet; follows E. all the way to Rouen; proposes marriage and is told to have patience; when she visits his home and he says he knows the truth about her family already she accepts; they are married; she discovers in the grounds of his estate a cottage where another woman lives, described as Viscountess Mountclere, but her husband thwarts her attempt to run away and says that the other woman has gone; E. stays; they settle; she manages him firmly and he is happy.

NEIGH, ALFRED, man about town in his mid-thirties, supercilious guest at the dinner party where Ethelberta sings; it turns out he is secretly in love with E. who is struck by him because of his detached manner towards her (one man who does not automatically fall at her feet); he twice suggests marriage to her; she asks for time; he meets her in Rouen and he, too, is told to wait.

*****PETHERWIN, ETHELBERTA**, born in humble circumstances, wooed by a rich young man who dies on the honeymoon; widowed at 17, she is taken in by her mother-in-law Lady Petherwin provided she keeps quiet about her family, a condition in which she (and her family) acquiesce; now 21, she is 'a pretty piece', tall, auburn-haired, self-possessed, confident, and strong-willed; she has just published an acclaimed volume of poetry; she meets by chance Christopher Julian who once courted her and she sends him her poems; she sets up a one-woman show in London, telling tall tales she has devised herself which attract good audiences and good notices; after her mother-in-law dies and leaves her only the house but no money, she moves in her numerous siblings as domestic staff, takes in French lodgers and sets up the shows to keep finances going; she increasingly ponders her uncertain future and the need to support a large family, thus feels Neigh's reported idea of seeking her hand might be politic, she twice asks for time; both her parents warn her that the position is becoming precarious (any report of a bold independent career woman from the *servant* class would kill her livelihood); she dines with Lord Mountclere who is so struck with her he follows her to Rouen; Ladywell and Neigh also arrive there and are told to wait; Mountclere also proposes marriage and is likewise told to wait; E. resists an impulse to seek the easy way out by taking him immediately, and gets depressed at the future; she is invited to Mountclere's stately home, he asks again and when he reveals he knew about her background already, she accepts; they are married; she finds a cottage in his grounds where lives a woman said to be Lady Mountclere; furiously, she tries to escape to France but is thwarted by her husband who says that the other has gone anyway, and from now on E. will be his mistress and queen; she shows a will of iron, with all her skills she returns his estates to profitability, sees her family is all taken care of, and in the library of her mansion she begins an epic poem.

PETHERWIN, LADY, widow of City man Sir Ralph; she is impetuous, wealthy and snobbish; she presses Ethelberta without success to suppress her poems as 'disloyal' to her son's memory; irritated by this, she alters her will, leaving E. only her house and furniture; dies while on holiday in Switzerland.

TIPMAN, trusted valet to Lord Mountclere, tells his employer what he has learned about E's background and is given cash to keep it quiet; he marries Menlove.

JUDE THE OBSCURE

There are two women in the life of gentle stonemason Jude Fawley, Arabella whom he marries and Sue whom he loves, while he seeks vainly to become a student at the university. The two women interweave with his quest; Jude dies young, sad and unfulfilled.

*****BRIDEHEAD, SUE,** widely read, free-thinking, broad-minded, atheist (until circumstances overwhelm her); very daringly lived with an undergraduate before the story opens; dark-haired, petite, pretty and in her mid-twenties when she meets Jude, her first cousin, while working as an artist in a shop selling artefacts;

i) at Jude's suggestion she becomes an assistant in Phillotson's village school; she is expelled from a teachers' training college for meeting Jude after hours; she marries Phillotson but does not love him; she leaves him to go and live with Jude in a platonic relationship; after Jude's son Father Time is dumped on them they set out for a register office to marry but do not go through with the ceremony because they feel they ought never 'to have come together for the most preposterous of all joint-ventures *for them* – matrimony'.

ii) the next four years they have a happy full relationship and a son and daughter are born to them; they face growing prejudice because their relationship is questioned and then because of the size of their family; the turning point comes when the family once again seeks new accommodation: Jude, a heavily pregnant Sue, and three small children are turned away; Father Time kills his two half-siblings and himself; the same night Sue is delivered of a stillborn child; overcome with guilt and crushed in spirit, she forces herself to remarry Phillotson, despite her repugnance, and stays on 'tired and miserable'.

CARTLETT, Mr, pot-bellied pub landlord, marries Arabella in Australia while she is still legally married to Jude; they come to England, where they hope to take a pub in Lambeth. Alcoholic Cartlett dies, Arabella turns to Jude for help.

***DONN, ARABELLA,** barmaid 'of rank passions', with a fine brown complexion and 'round and prominent bosom'; coarse, vulgar and with a strong-eye for the main chance, but not a good picker, all three men she chooses are losers; daughter of a pig-breeder who helps her father with cleaning offal; makes Jude's acquaintance by playfully flinging a pig's penis at his head as he passes by; he is 19 and she seduces him, traps him into marriage and leaves him after two months; Arabella emigrates to Australia where she gives birth to Jude's son and marries bigamously; comes back to England to start a pub business with her new man and parks on Jude their son, Father Time; pub business fails, her publican husband dies and she comes to Jude destitute asking for help; taking her in out of pity, she gets him hooked on drink and gets him to remarry her, but soon resents decline in his health; she takes up with Physician Vilbert even before Jude is dead and attends Jude's funeral with Widow Edlin.

EDLIN, the WIDOW, neighbour and friend of Drusilla Fawley; tends her in her last illness; comes to act as a witness at the wedding ceremony of Jude and Sue which comes to nothing, contrasting this with her own wedding some 55 years before when the feasting lasted a week and she had to borrow half-a-crown to set up house with her husband; she and Arabella are the only mourners at Jude's funeral.

FAWLEY, DRUSILLA, great-aunt of Jude Fawley, owner of a village bakery, who reluctantly takes in the orphaned child, gets him his first job as bird scarer, afterwards he acts as her bread delivery man; later she vigorously advises Jude against marriage with Sue and says that members of her family make bad marriages – a prediction which turns out to be highly prescient.

***FAWLEY, JUDE,** a sensitive orphan, is reluctantly taken in by his great-aunt Drusilla when he is 11, his first job is to scare crows off the produce of a local farmer but he is thrashed and sacked after the farmer hears him encouraging the birds to feed instead of scaring them;

i) he bids farewell to his mentor, the schoolmaster Phillotson, who is setting out to become a student at the university, an aim Jude seeks later to emulate (with no more success than Phillotson has); Jude acts as deliveryman for his aunt's bakery, then becomes a respected stonemason who at one time is specifically invited back by a former employer;

ii) at 19 he meets barmaid Arabella who gets him drunk and traps him into marriage; she leaves him after two months. Jude goes to the university town of Christminster (Oxford) where he meets his cousin Sue and falls in love with her but feels restrained as he is already married; now in his early twenties, with thick black hair and a beard thick for a man his age, he has a gentle expression – one of several hints as to his Christlike character; he gets Sue a job as Phillotson's teaching assistant; she marries Phillotson but does not love him and comes to live with Jude permanently;

iii) Jude's son by Arabella (known as Little Father Time) comes to join them and a son and daughter are born to them; as Jude moves around the country for work they have growing accommodation problems, first because they are not married and then because of the nature of the family: a common artisan, a heavily pregnant woman and three small children; Father Time kills his two half-siblings, then himself; Sue is delivered of a stillborn child the same night;

iv) overwhelmed, Sue leaves Jude to go back to Phillotson; Arabella comes to Jude for help when she is destitute, he takes her in and she feeds him drink until he remarries her, then resents his failing health and takes up with Physician Philbert while Jude is dying; Arabella and Widow Edlin attend Jude's funeral: he is not yet in his 30th year, so his narrative covers about 18 years.

GILLINGHAM, GEORGE, schoolteacher and childhood friend who gives loyal support to Phillotson but in debate on his friend's marriage vigorously defends traditional values; acts as best man when Phillotson remarries Sue.

FATHER TIME, LITTLE, Jude's son by Arabella; pale, wide-eyed, withdrawn, placid boy with 'a face like the muse of Greek tragedy'; a child born in Australia who no-one wants; dispatched by his mother to Jude and Sue, quickly calls Sue mother but remains remote; as situation of Jude and Sue gets progressively more desperate, first because they are not married and then because no landlady wants to take them in, kills his two half-siblings, then himself, leaving a note: 'Done because we are too many'.

PHILLOTSON, RICHARD, country schoolmaster who says farewell to the boy Jude to set out for Christminster (Oxford) in unsuccessful bid to become a student just as Jude does some years later; instead starts running a school again and at Jude's instigation takes on Sue as his assistant; she enters into a loveless marriage with him; she leaves him to live with Jude, because of which he loses his school post for 'giving his wife her freedom'; he goes back to his former village but is forced to take a low-paid job; he remarries Sue – who, typically, he calls Susanna – but the marriage is not consummated until after she meets Jude again.

TROUTHAM, FARMER, gives the 11-year-old Jude his first job as bird-scarer but when he finds that the boy is encouraging the crows to eat his produce instead of scaring them away gives him a thrashing and dismisses him.

VILBERT, called PHYSICIAN, itinerant pedlar of love potions and other quack remedies, promises to help Jude with books but lets him down; when Jude lies dying Arabella sees him as the next man to latch on to.

A LAODICEAN

Wealthy Paula Power has two suitors, soldier William de Stancy and architect George Somerset. De Stancy's illegitimate son seeks to promote his father's cause by blackening Somerset's character; the truth comes out and Somerset wins the lady.

BELL, BARBARA, 35, of Regent's Theatre, London, agrees to take Paula Power's lead role in 'Love's Labour's Lost' at a few hours' notice for a fee of 50 guineas.

DARE, Willy, 'a graceless lad', illegitimate son of Captain de Stancy with DE STANCY tattooed on his chest, hired by George Somerset as an architectural assistant after he has purloined and destroyed letters from other applicants; soon dismissed for incompetence; induces competing architect Havill to copy Somerset's plans; encourages his father to drink alcohol again and spurs his latent sexual desire by pressing him to marry Paula Power; undermines Somerset by sending a begging letter to Paula in his name from Monte Carlo and with a trick photo which appears to show Somerset drunk; back in England, Paula's lost uncle Abner Power tries to blackmail Dare, but as he knows about Power's own dubious past and revolvers are produced, the meeting is a draw; when Dare's tricks are discovered his father refuses to turn him in; in the end a mysterious figure is seen setting Stancy Castle ablaze.

HAZE, CUNNINGHAM, local chief constable, tells George Somerset he saw men in his studio late one night; Somerset rightly suspects illicit entry by Havill and Dare and digs out a photo of Dare to prove the point to Haze but passes it to Captain de Stancy instead of to Haze; de Stancy recognises the picture as that of his son and destroys it.

DE STANCY, CHARLOTTE, plump and plain, early twenties, companion to Paula Power; daughter of Sir William and sister of Captain de Stancy; secretly in love with George Somerset; after Paula's marriage she enters a nunnery.

DE STANCY, Captain William, Royal Horse Artillery, dour and much travelled soldier, 39, tanned face, raven black hair and beard, Dare's father; confessing vulnerability to pretty women, he is entranced when he secretly watches Paula Power doing callisthenic exercises; acts opposite her in a play and falls in love with her; eventually she accepts him 'out of pity' but on the morning of the wedding the exposure of Dare and his father's refusal to turn him in leads to Paula sending him away; he leaves the area with his regiment.

DE STANCY, SIR WILLIAM, baronet, forced to sell Stancy Castle after spendthrift youth, now lives modestly in nearby villa and stresses the values of frugality.

GOODMAN, MRS, recently widowed aunt of Paula Power who has come to live at Stancy Castle as her chaperone and travel companion.

HAVILL, surly, bearded, elderly one-time road contractor who has set himself up as architect; designed the local 'monstrosity' nonconformist chapel; shows in discussion with George Somerset a poor grasp of architectural history; cheats to get share of castle contract but renounces it after his wife dies and he develops pangs of conscience; he is reengaged on a limited contract after Somerset stands down.

POWER, ABNER, grey-faced 'queer elderly foreigner', a one-time anarchist with a face scarred by explosive; comes to see his niece Paula, plants in local press a bogus story that Captain de Stancy may be marrying her; Abner takes her abroad on a holiday; a week before the scheduled marriage between Paula and the captain he meets Dare and the two threaten to expose each other's pasts, but as they both produce a revolver the meeting is a draw; Power goes back abroad.

***POWER, PAULA,** early twenties, abundant brown hair, with 'cheerful beauty and brightness of intellect', has inherited Stancy Castle from her father, an MP, wealthy railway contractor and staunch Baptist; she now opposes joining the local nonconformist congregation; she offends the local minister Mr Woodwell by holding back from going through a baptism ceremony in the new chapel; commissions George Somerset to refurbish the castle; when he declares his love she refuses to commit herself; she takes the lead role in amateur production of 'Love's Labour's Lost' but stands down for a second performance; hears Somerset's repeated avowal but keeps him at a distance; she does the same with de Stancy but later agrees to marry him 'out of pity'; on the morning of the wedding Charlotte reveals the Dare plot; Paula sends de Stancy away and goes in pursuit of Somerset to make amends; when she finds him she tells him to propose to her.

SOMERSET, GEORGE, architect, is commissioned by heiress Paula Power to refurbish West Country Stancy Castle for a £100,000 contract; he is 25, a 'nice young man' with a good moustache but his beard is wispy; a bit of a pedant but knowledgeable, holding his own in theological debate with Baptist preacher Woodwell and crushing charlatan Havill in discussion on architecture; confesses his love for Paula Power; much upset when Captain de Stancy acts opposite her and apparently kisses her on stage but she tells him their lips were kept an inch apart because she has never been kissed; after Dare's trick in sending a begging letter in his name he is distressed by her coldness and eventually quits the assignment; when the truth comes out Paula comes to search for him; they marry.

SOMERSET, Mr, portrait painter and RA, asks his son George to undertake for him a commission to design costumes for a production of 'Love's Labour's Lost', by coincidence the one at Stancy Castle; later goes on a tour of Normandy with his son.

WOODWELL, REV., kindly old nonconformist preacher horrified when Paula Power refuses to proceed with baptism ceremony, reproaching her with 'thou art neither cold nor hot: I would thou wert cold or hot'. {*A key to the novel's title is this quote from the Book of Revelations 3, in which inhabitants of Laodicea are dismissed as lacking commitment*}.

THE MAYOR OF CASTERBRIDGE

Hardy's subtitle: "The Life and Death of a Man of Character"

***FARFRAE, DONALD**, a migrant from the Edinburgh region, 5ft 9in and lightly built, fair-haired, bright-eyed, is passing through Casterbridge to go abroad when he is impulsively engaged by Mayor Henchard to put his business straight; takes charge capably so quickly that he moves Henchard to talk about his personal affairs; under Farfrae's management, the firm prospers and following the Whittle incident Farfrae becomes the real force; he becomes aware of the budding beauty of Elizabeth-Jane; he organises a successful Céilidh in a tent to entertain Casterbridge townsfolk and dances with Elizabeth-Jane; he sets up in business on his own after being impulsively sacked by Henchard and straightaway he is successful; he becomes struck with Lucetta, marries her, takes over Henchard's business and becomes mayor; Lucetta dies; he marries Elizabeth-Jane.

HENCHARD, MICHAEL, is the Mayor of Casterbridge; first appearance is as hay-trusser, well-built, swarthy, 6ft 1 1/2in, gets fiercely drunk at a country fair and, dissatisfied with the fact that he tied himself down by marrying at 18, puts his wife Susan and baby daughter up for auction and sells them to a sailor for five guineas; when he later regrets his action he takes an oath not to drink for 20 years; scene shifts 18 years on and Henchard has a rich complexion and harsh laugh, a hard man knowing no moderation in his requests and impulses; he is mayor of a town living from farming; he is the biggest merchant and friendly with its bankers; he presides at a dinner of top burgesses where he is much criticised for a racket selling poor-quality wheat but he swears he was not to blame; he meets Donald Farfrae and impulsively appoints him manager; Farfrae starts immediately on putting chaotic business papers in order; Henchard takes him into his confidence and tells him of his past, including links with a woman in Jersey; that very day the wife of Henchard's youth who has fallen on hard times and sought out her husband meets him – he acknowledges her but has to move carefully, setting her up shortly afterwards in a cottage; meanwhile Henchard has told Farfrae he wants to remarry Susan but he has in the meanwhile become involved with a Jersey woman; at his request Farfrae drafts for his new boss a letter dismissing the woman with a cheque; he gives Farfrae a free hand in the business and it flourishes, but after the Whittle incident Farfrae is *de facto* boss; when Farfrae intends to arrange a public entertainment Henchard wants to outshine him and sets up an expensive fair with sideshows in an open field but it is rained off, while Farfrae's much more modest effort is held in a sturdy tent with music and reels that is a huge success; Henchard, humiliated, sacks Farfrae, who buys his own business; Henchard finds his affairs declining not only because of the increased competition but because his standing has declined; his wife Susan dies and he tells Elizabeth-Jane that he is her father and she must so regard him, but he goes upstairs to get some papers to prove it and finds instead a letter by Susan explaining that this Elizabeth-Jane is her child by sailor Newson, the first child having died after the wife-sale; Henchard so fears loss of face he does not tell the girl, who now calls him father; the one-time Jersey friend Lucetta comes to live in Casterbridge to revive the relationship; he hangs back initially, she falls for Farfrae, he pressures her and with Elizabeth-Jane present asks her again to marry him: she accepts – and promptly faints with revulsion; he is publicly humiliated when a woman had up in the magistrate's court on a minor charge says that she recognises the chairman of the bench as the man who sold his wife 20 years before; public knowledge of his past is a crushing blow to his standing and his business; on the outskirts of town Lucetta and Elizabeth-Jane are threatened by an angry bull but Henchard happens to be near; always physically strong and never lacking physical courage, he grabs the animal by the ring on its nose and saves them; when Lucetta says she is grateful he asks if in return she might help him because his business is tottering but she tells him she cannot as she has just married Farfrae; Henchard is declared bankrupt; he gets employment from Farfrae as a labourer in the granary he once owned; 20 years of his abstinence oath being up he starts drinking again and is filled with growing hatred for Farfrae; Lucetta begs him to return the Jersey letters; he entrusts them to Jopp with unexpected results; Henchard waylays Farfrae, challenges him to a fight, wins but hangs back from administering the coup de grâce; the sailor Newson appears and asks for his daughter but Henchard, fearful of losing Elizabeth-Jane whom he has now come to need, says she is dead; he soon regrets the lie but the sailor has gone; he looks over a bridge parapet contemplating suicide and sees floating into view the effigy of him made for the skimity-ride which so mocked him and Lucetta publicly; shocked, he feels his life has been saved; Elizabeth-Jane moves in with him, they are set up in a small shop and are happy; slowly he sees romance growing between Elizabeth-Jane and Farfrae and when Newson comes into view again he feels his emotional life is crumbling, so he dons hay-trusser garb again and leaves Casterbridge in the way he was when he first came there; he falls ill and is sheltered and tended by Abel Whittle until he dies.

HENCHARD, SUSAN, married very young; she has extreme simplicity of intellect and can do no more than write her own name; when the sailor who bought her is reported lost at sea and leaves her poor she traces Henchard and finds he is now a man of substance; the mayor rents a cottage for her; he 'remarries' Susan to make things look right for Elizabeth-Jane and installs them in his house; Susan remains as self-effacing as ever; she falls ill and dies, leaving a letter explaining that her child by Henchard died early and that the present Elizabeth-Jane is her child by Newson.

JOPP, JOSHUA, comes up for interview as Henchard's manager of the granary as arranged earlier but much to his anger is summarily dismissed and told the job has been taken by Farfrae; Henchard hires him again after sacking Farfrae but when his summer gamble on harvests goes badly wrong he unfairly blames Jopp and dismisses him again; Henchard, obliged to take lodgings with Jopp, asks him to deliver to Lucetta letters of their Jersey relationship she has asked for; Jopp wants revenge, and in a drinking den has the letters read; wayward characters plan a cruel reprisal of a skimity-ride, a public humiliation.

NEWSON, ELIZABETH-JANE, Susan's daughter, is 18 and pretty, bears the sailor's surname and knows nothing of the wife-sale; countrified, withdrawn, shy; falls in love with Farfrae but loses him to Lucetta; at one stage runs a shop with her stepfather Henchard, who has wrongly told her he is her real father; after Lucetta dies Farfrae turns to her again, she is happily married to him and also reunited with her biological father.

NEWSON, CAPTAIN RICHARD, stoutly-built sailor with broad and genial face and grey whiskers; comes back 20 years after the wife-sale looking for his daughter; Henchard lies and says she is dead; he leaves but when he returns more than a year later he meets her in Farfrae's house and the truth is soon established; he pays for the drinks at the happy wedding of his daughter with Donald Farfrae.

***TEMPLEMAN, LUCETTA,** is a dark-haired bright-eyed well-educated young Jersey woman of unmistakably French descent; before the novel begins she nurses Henchard who has fallen ill in St Helier while on business; he promises to marry her; when Susan reappears he brusquely dismisses her with a letter and a cheque; when she reads that Susan has died, and as she has meanwhile inherited money, sets up in a fine house in Casterbridge to re-establish relations as she feels her past has been compromised by Henchard; he is not very forthcoming and when she meets Farfrae is far more taken with him (he is after all more her own age), so Lucetta and Elizabeth-Jane become rivals for Farfrae; Henchard comes round and proposes marriage but she has cooled, so Henchard and Farfrae become rivals for Lucetta; Henchard persists and eventually she accepts but immediately faints; she hears the truth about the wife-sale and is miserable; while out walking outside town with Elizabeth-Jane they are threatened by an angry bull; Henchard is near and with great presence of mind saves the women from danger; she says she is grateful and he asks her for help in return as his business is in trouble, but she says she cannot as she has just married Farfrae, revelation of the wife-sale having made Henchard unacceptable in her eyes; she moves with Farfrae into Henchard's old mansion; Mr and Mrs Farfrae become the town's top couple; Farfrae is out of the house when she hears a tumult in the street outside – it is a parade of large stuffed unmistakable caricatures of Lucetta and Henchard, bound back to back mounted on a donkey passing through town being jeered at by the populace – a skimity-ride, traditional way of mocking adulterers; she faints in arms of Elizabeth-Jane, dies of a miscarriage.

WHITTLE, ABEL, simple-minded young comic rustic ('Poor Abel'), often warned about being late for work; one morning it happens again and exasperated Henchard goes to his lodgings to fetch him and sends him to the granary without his trousers on; Farfrae sees him arrive and tells him to dress and when Henchard says no Farfrae threatens to quit; Henchard gives way and from then on Farfrae dominates the firm; when Farfrae has his own firm, Abel is given a job and 'tis better for us than 'twas'; two years later he comes across Henchard in a bad way in the countryside, gives him shelter and selfless care until the one-time mayor dies.

A PAIR OF BLUE EYES

A romance of the girl who got away. Blue-eyed country maiden Elfride tires of two suitors, neither of whom comes up to the mark, and settles for someone perhaps more suitable...

CANNISTER, MARTIN, good-humoured sexton, brings home Stephen Smith's luggage, attends party for the homecoming from India; helps prepare Lady Luxellian's tomb; takes over Welcome Home pub and marries Elfride's maid Unity.

JETHWAY, GERTRUDE, a crazed and forlorn widow badly-disposed towards Elfride Swancourt because she (unjustly) blames Elfride for the death of her farmer son Felix who was said to love the girl; she is killed when the church tower collapses but in a note from beyond the grave not only tells Henry Knight the main facts about Elfride's elopement, but makes it look as if Knight is third, not second, in the list of Elfride's lovers.

***KNIGHT, HENRY** (Suitor Number 2), 30, dark brown hair, curly beard and crisp moustache, earnest and puritanical magazine essayist who is hero-worshipped by Stephen Smith (Suitor number 1), in whom he takes a patronising interest; as a distant relation of Mrs Troyton's he is invited on her remarriage to visit her and her new husband Swancourt; meets Elfride and in a clifftop mishap pushes her to safety, Elfride in turn saves his life by pulling him over with a rope made from her underwear; by the time Stephen Smith returns from India, Henry has achieved total ascendancy over Elfride; he makes it plain that as he has never been kissed the woman he marries must be the same; from Mrs Jethway and elsewhere the truth inevitably emerges and he walks out immediately because of 'my taste...for untried lips'.

Henry tours the Continent, comes back and meets Stephen Smith by chance in London; Henry learns for the first time who Elfride's lover was, the elopement and all its consequences; the old friendship has cooled; each tries to steal a march on the other by travelling west, but their paths cross again and, anyway, find they are only just in time for Elfride's funeral; the two suitors walk off disconsolately.

LICKPAN, MARTIN, pig-killer, attends the party for Stephen's homecoming; has fund of stories about pigs he has slaughtered.

LORD LUXELLIAN, 15th baron, muddle-headed landowner with a pleasant laugh but no ability; helps Henry Knight to carry away the body of Mrs Jethway; marries Elfride as company for his daughters.

LADY LUXELLIAN, his first wife, peeress with a watery look and a poor taste in jewellery; dies at 31.

LUXELLIAN, MARY and KATE, affectionate small daughters of Lord and Lady Luxellian; much attached to Elfride Swancourt because she is kinder to them than their mother is.

SMITH, JANE, wife of John, a woman of sound common sense, says it is too early for her son Stephen to marry but that he might very well do better than a mere parson's daughter; she comments that class distinctions are eroding.

SMITH, JOHN, master-mason living near Endelstow rectory, man of stalwart healthiness with ruddy arms, so much better off than the Swancourts that he can afford to have his son Stephen enter 'an expensive profession'.

***SMITH, STEPHEN** (Suitor Number 1), 'a youth in appearance but not yet a man', aged just over 20, handsome with red lips, and light brown fuzz on the upper lip; courteous, considerate, gentle; trainee architect sent from London to prepare for restoration of Endelstow church; stays with clergyman Swancourt; Stephen and Swancourt's daughter Elfride fall in love but the young man is rebuffed by the rector when he is revealed to be of humble birth; he returns to London but arranges secret marriage in Plymouth; he messes up the marriage licence and the couple are forced to elope to London for the ceremony but Elfride returns home with objective unattained; Stephen goes to Bombay for a year, comes back and she fails to meet him as promised; he finds her with Knight and is too diffident to speak out even though she has brusquely returned his gift of £200; he goes back to India and does well; back in London he meets Henry Knight and at last the full story of the elopement comes out; the two men each try to get to Elfride in the west separately and meet on the train anyway, but they come in time only for her funeral.

***SWANCOURT, ELFRIDE, 19 or 20, but with manner of a girl of 15, pretty with fine blue eyes, falls in love with visiting architect Stephen Smith; after her father's rejection of Stephen as a suitor agrees to marry him secretly in Plymouth, but because the licence is made out for London the couple must go there; in London Elfride gets cold feet and returns home; her romantic novel about the time of King Arthur gets mixed reviews including a heavy-going one in Knight's journal; just before he arrives to visit at her stepmother's invitation, Elfride is much more struck by Knight's criticism of her book than by the endearments in Stephen Smith's letter from Bombay; she is gradually drawn to Knight as a heavyweight compared with Stephen, 'hardly enough of a man'; when her two suitors at last meet Knight introduces Elfride to Smith as his fiancée and neither Smith nor Elfride reveals the truth; having run out on one lover Elfride is confronted the next day by widow Jethway who accuses her of running out on her dead son as well and says she spotted Elfride coming back from London after 'playing the wife' with Smith; the more Henry lays down the law about chastity the more her fears grow; inevitably the truth comes out, largely through the malign Mrs Jethway; Henry walks out, she follows him desperately to get him back without success; time goes by;

after her two suitors have met in London they both independently travel west to mend fences: they are too late – Elfride married Lord Luxellian and died of a miscarriage.

SWANCOURT, the Rev. CHRISTOPHER. Rector of Endelstow in Lower Wessex, 50, genial temperament and hearty voice; is appalled by his daughter's desire to marry someone of humble birth, but not so appalled when he has the chance to marry a widow of humble birth with £3,500 a year; later it is revealed that Swancourt's first wife was the granddaughter of a Lord Luxellian and that the rector had eloped with her, so history had been repeating itself; when Elfride and Henry split up, he follows Elfride to London and accuses Henry of caddishness.

TROYTON, CHARLOTTE, dark, pretty, good-humoured widow with a low, musical voice; she has estate in the country and in London; marries Swancourt secretly, two elopements with the same aim but different result.

UNITY, maid to Elfride, has a very good memory as to what her mistress does with her earrings; marries the sexton and runs a pub.

WORM, WILLIAM, loyal, feeble-minded manservant to Christopher Swancourt; much troubled by noise in his ears *(nowadays probably seen as tinnitus)*.

THE RETURN OF THE NATIVE

Story set entirely in the 'heathy, furzy, briary wilderness' of Egdon, where Eustacia Vye, a woman with hot Mediterranean blood who stops at nothing to get the men she wants, may overreach herself...

NUNSUCH, SUSAN, countrywoman, stabs Eustacia with a stocking needle in church to stop her bewitching her children; Eustacia, who is in ill repute among heath people because of her uninhibited ways, faints but soon recovers; when Mrs Yeobright is bitten by an adder on the heath Susan brings a frying pan to produce the fat to cure the bite by frying adders; her son Johnny makes a chance remark to Clym which leads him to discover Eustacia rejected his mother; Johnny falls seriously ill, and Susan sees Eustacia, shapes her in a beeswax effigy and sticks pins into it before burning it mumbling a magic incantation; a few hours later Eustacia drowns.

VENN, DIGGORY *(reddleman by trade, tours Egdon Heath selling farmers red dye to mark ewes that have been mated)*; tall, blue-eyed, clean-shaven, a fine figure of a man of 24 in his tight-fitting corduroys, but because of his work he is red from head to foot – clothes, cap, face; a patient, kindly man who is in love with Thomasin whom he takes back home after her wedding to Wildeve, a man he despises has been botched; in June he keeps a check on Wildeve whom he mistrusts, and one evening after the innkeeper has won a fortune in gold coins in a dice game on the heath from a country yokel, which Mrs Yeobright had entrusted the youth to carry to Clym and Thomasin, he challenges Wildeve to another game and on the lonely heath in the midnight silence – illumined only by glowworms – he wins the hundred guineas back for the family; the night of Eustacia's elopement he plays a leading part in the rescue operation; time goes by, he gives up his profitable business to buy a dairy farm, cleans himself up and dresses in a smart bottle-green coat to go a-courting – and so he marries his true love Thomasin.

***VYE, EUSTACIA**, tall, black-haired, daughter of a Corfu musician, lives with her grandfather on Egdon Heath, which she loathes – she yearns for bright lights; she knows Wildeve is a trifler but she loves him because love is the only cordial against loneliness; a rebellious woman whose eyes glow with triumphant pleasure when the bonfire she lights on 5 November succeeds in her aim of luring him back now that his wedding to Thomasin has just come to naught.

i) Wildeve to Yeobright: Eustacia hears Mrs Yeobright's son Clym is returning from Paris and this fires her imagination so much she inveigles herself into a party of mummers presenting a folk play in the Yeobrights' home at Christmas, so that in her disguise she can glimpse this man who 'is the first she has ever been inclined to adore' and when he speaks kindly to her later she is 'warmed with inner fire'; some weeks later heathwoman Susan Nunsuch stabs Eustacia with a stocking needle because she believes she is bewitching her children; Eustacia marries Clym on 25 June and within a month vainly begins to pressure him to go to Paris: 'I warned you I had not good wifely qualities'; he clings to the heath work he is limited to because of his sight and she reflects, 'two wasted lives – his and mine';

ii) Yeobright to Wildeve: to cheer herself up she goes to a village dance where she meets Wildeve again – old feelings are revived; while Wildeve is visiting her cottage Mrs Yeobright calls and Eustacia does not open the door; when Clym discovers this he reproaches Eustacia, accuses her and she walks out; she goes back to her grandfather; another 5 November, another bonfire, another tryst – she begs Wildeve to take her away; the next day they set off for a new life but in crossing a rain-swollen weir they both drown. (*In classic tradition, action for the central figure spans just a year and a day*).

WILDEVE, DAMON, youthful, graceful, reduced to innkeeping through fecklessness; botches licence arrangements to marry Thomasin, goes back to his base, the Quiet Woman Inn; that evening he sees Eustacia's bonfire and so only hours after the wedding that never was finds it impossible to resist the lure of his former love; weeks later he marries Thomasin; in late summer he goes to a village festivity and dances all evening with Eustacia; he inherits £11,000 and tells her he plans to visit Paris – which excites her; on 5 November he meets her by a bonfire again, she tells how unhappy she is and he promises her anything she wants; at her behest they depart but when crossing a weir they both drown.

YEOBRIGHT, CLYM, aged about 30, is the Egdon native who returns from being manager of a diamond firm in Paris for the Christmas holiday; he tells his mother he will not go back but be a schoolmaster as he has no ambition left and finds the diamond trade idle and vain; he meets Eustacia and is soon attracted, so dividing his time between schoolbooks and seeing her clandestinely; *he* wants to set up a school with her help, *she* wants him take her to Paris; he sees conflict in aims but still they marry on 25 June and find a lonely heath cottage; the honeymoon period is short-lived, firstly because he has no intention of taking his bride to Paris and secondly because his intensive studies have brought such severe eye strain he becomes a semi-invalid with dark glasses; the only work he can do is as a poorly paid furze-cutter on the heath, which fits perfectly with his new mood but adds to Eustacia's frustration; not knowing of his mother's vain visit earlier he goes to mend fences and on his way to his mother's finds her suffering from adder-bite; heathfolk try to help her recovery with snake oil but in vain; he is ill with remorse for weeks, when he learns the truth about Eustacia's keeping the door closed against his mother, there are violent reproaches and mutual accusations; Eustacia walks out; after her death he lives as a recluse but finally finds a new purpose in life as an itinerant preacher throughout Wessex.

YEOBRIGHT, Mrs, widely-respected quiet-spoken widow; fiercely protective of her niece Thomasin; in November she fails to prevent her going to marry Wildeve; when the wedding collapses because of his mistake she goes to his inn to protest unsuccessfully because she feels Thomasin's honour has been compromised and takes the girl home; she is distressed when her son Clym comes from Paris for Christmas and tells her he will quit successful Paris job; she is appalled at Eustacia – 'a voluptuous, idle woman'; there is a rift after the marriage which on 31 August she tries to breach – she walks to Clym's cottage but Eustacia does not open the door; Mrs Yeobright is shattered at rejection and on the way back home is bitten by an adder; Clym and heathfolk find her and fry adders to produce the fat that would be a cure, but the walk has been too much for her heart.

YEOBRIGHT, THOMASIN, fair, sweet ingénue with wavy chestnut hair, rejected Venn's marriage proposal two years ago because of opposition from her aunt; lately fascinated by plausible publican Wildeve, and angry at his bungling the wedding licence; but she marries him a few weeks later. He takes her to his home, the remote Quiet Woman Inn; he is mean and neglectful; she bears him a daughter he calls Eustacia; after Wildeve's death she marries Venn.

TESS OF THE D'URBERVILLES

Hardy's subtitle: 'A pure woman'

***CLARE, ANGEL,** student on a walking holiday in the heart of the country sees May-Day dancers and joins in, but does not pick local village girl Tess though their eyes meet; three years later he is learning to do milking at big Talbothayes dairy as part of training to become a farmer; at 26 he has something nebulous, preoccupied and vague in his bearing, with a delicate mouth and light moustache and beard; he is an unskilled milker and a mediocre harp player; falls in love with Tess and sees himself as a man of principle who has to move slowly; to his family he describes Tess as a cottager's daughter, beautiful and 'virtuous as a vestal' but his clergyman father wants him to marry the (genteel) girl next door; Angel goes back to the dairy, proposes to Tess and she weeps, 'never, never'; he keeps pressing her; she accepts him and just before the wedding he hears a passing stranger who apparently knows Tess's background make derogatory remarks about her; Angel knocks the man down, but the incident triggers her decision to tell him of her past immediately but he light-heartedly keeps asking her not to; when she tells him on the wedding night of her child he is shocked and sharply rejects her; despite his urge to be a free thinker, he is 'slave to custom and conventionality'; they split; he sets off to go farming in Brazil and when he meets milkmaid Izz Huett asks her to join him and she accepts; when she tells him Tess would willingly have died for him he changes his mind; in Brazil he falls ill; comes back worn and haggard; receives Tess's message and goes to seek her; finds her in a smart villa; she tells him bitterly he is too late as she has 'yielded to him' (Alec); he leaves and finds her later catching him up on foot, saying she has killed Alec; he takes complete charge, protecting her as they keep out of the way deep in the country; Tess says her sister Liza-Lu is pure and good and would make him a good wife; they come to

Stonehenge where they are seized by a posse of 16 men; after the trial Angel and Liza-Lu wait outside the prison to see the signal that the death sentence has been carried out.

***D'URBERVILLE, ALEC,** son of nouveau riche merchant who purchased the D'Urberville surname some years ago to add some sparkle to his original surname of Stoke (so there is no link between this spurious house and the Durbeyfields); Alec is in his early twenties, swarthy with a well-groomed black moustache with curled points; he greets Tess with, 'Well, my big Beauty', a clear reference to her well-developed figure; he repeatedly makes passes at her while she runs his mother's poultry-house and she always fights him off; later that summer he finds her on her way home from a night out with some farmworkers; she is involved in an altercation and he puts her behind him on his horse; he rides homeward with her in thick fog; in a lonely spot he drugs her; she falls asleep; he achieves his aim; when she is pregnant and decides to walk back home he offers help which she rejects; he says of himself: 'I was born bad, and I have lived bad, and I shall die bad in all probability'; over three years later he is a preacher, converted by Angel's father the evangelical Rev. Clare; when he meets Tess he changes rapidly blaming her for his 'backsliding'; he presses her to go off with him, offers marriage and when he learns of her marriage refers to Angel as 'that mule of a husband'; she strikes him with her heavy leather working glove and draws blood; her situation worsens and when he rescues her mother and siblings from poverty she moves in with him; Angel appears and she tells Alec tearfully she has sent him away; he makes a coarse remark about Angel; Tess takes a carving knife and stabs Alec in the heart.

D'URBERVILLE, MRS, Alec's mother and widow of the businessman who bought the bogus surname; she is silver-haired, blind, not yet 60; loves her only child resentfully and is 'bitterly fond'.

DURBEYFIELD, JOHN (Jack), alcoholic and feckless deliveryman; he and his wife Joan have seven surviving children – Tess, Abraham, daughters Eliza-Louisa (Liza-Lu), Hope and Modesty, a boy of three and a baby one year old; when parson Tringham tells him of the family's ancient history and greets him as 'Sir John' it goes to his head; he goes celebrating at Rolliver's alehouse with his wife and so is incapable of a vital overnight delivery which Tess has to undertake in his stead, losing the horse and so leading to her approaching the D'Urbervilles. When she comes back with her child and tells her father she wishes to have it baptised, Jack refuses to let her call a clergyman as he claims the family grandeur has been diminished; he dies and as occupancy of the family cottage reverts to the owner his family is left homeless.

DURBEYFIELD, JOAN, over-burdened with her husband, large family and dreary cottage, bitterly reproaches Tess for not handling matters better when she comes home pregnant; three years later when Tess writes about her forthcoming marriage she emphatically writes to Tess not to reveal her past; Tess comes home after four days of marriage and tells her what has happened and Joan reproaches her: 'you little fool'; when Joan becomes homeless she and her children are generously helped by Alec (as he seeks to win back Tess).

***DURBEYFIELD, TESS**, eldest child of Jack and Joan and the family's anchor of sensibility; a fine and handsome girl with bouncing womanliness, peony mouth and innocent eyes; 'a mere vessel of emotion untinctured by experience';

   i) She goes with the other girls of the village in the ritual May-Day dance; they are watched by three brothers on a walking holiday, the youngest is Angel Clare, who joins the dancers but does not pick Tess, but as he leaves they catch eyes; that evening her father is too drunk for an overnight delivery so she has to do it; following the death of the horse on which they depend to do their deliveries the family is even more on the edge of penury and Tess is therefore pressured to seek help at a place some miles way said to house a family called D'Urberville; she finds a handsome red brick mansion and is greeted by the cigar-smoking son of the house, a forward young man called Alec; he makes it plain he is much attracted to her but she does not feel he inspires trust; she gets a job there; when he tells her he has sent her siblings toys and her father a new horse, to win her over, her reaction is to burst into tears; after three months at the mansion she goes on a night out with some other farm girls, a quarrel breaks out as some drink has been taken; Tess arouses the ire of two girls who were apparently Alec's previous conquests; Alec happens to ride by, rescues her, and they lose their way in fog; in a lonely spot he drugs her, she falls asleep and, as the narrator puts it, 'where was Tess's guardian angel? Where was Providence?'; when she finds herself pregnant she quits her job and starts walking home; Alec catches up with her and says he will help any way she wants, including setting herself up for life, but she rejects it scornfully; he describes himself as a damn bad fellow; his parting line 20 to follow straight on...words are, 'good morning, my four months' cousin'; at home again a baby, a boy, is born; her father refuses her request to have the child baptised by a clergyman because having the matter become known would be a smudge on the family's new 'nobility'; the baby becomes sick and by candlelight and with the aid of the prayer book, her siblings kneeling round her, Tess in an ecstasy of faith baptises the dying child, naming him 'Sorrow'; she buries him in a poor part of the churchyard, fashions a cross from two sticks and places on the grave some flowers in a jar marked 'Keelwell's Marmalade';

ii) Time passes – at age 20 she is a mature personality, quickly established as a seasoned milkmaid at Talbothayes dairy farm; she meets trainee farmer Angel Clare; love grows gradually and when he proposes marriage she is devastated; eventually love overcomes her doubts, she accepts 31 December as her wedding date; some days before she writes Angel a four-page letter and slips it under his door; next day he is just the same; on her wedding morning she goes to check and sees the letter went not under his door but under the carpet; bitterly she tells Angel she wants to talk before the ceremony and he blithely tells her it can wait; on their wedding night he tells her about his London 'dissipation' with a woman and asks her to speak about her past; she says, 'perhaps it is as serious as yours', and tells him everything;

iii) His face slowly withers; he rejects her bitterly; they sleep apart, Tess going back to her mother; she drifts around; that winter hits a new low and has a job digging swedes in frozen soil; she is joined by friend Izz Huett and it comes out Angel asked Izz to come to Brazil with him; Tess is stung; decides to walk to home of Angel's parents to seek help but courage fails her at the last moment; on way home she passes a country barn crowded with people hearing a hellfire preacher; she recognises the voice at that of Alec; despite his new garb and voice she sees in him the same handsome unpleasantness of mien; he follows her and very soon changes back to ordinary clothes and accuses her of causing him to backslide; he pursues her now with vigour, proposes marriage; she refuses everything but when the family is further reduced and he helps generously she moves in with him to a villa; Angel appears, she tearfully tells him that it is all too late as 'I have yielded to him' even though she hates him; she goes in to tell Alec she has sent Angel away; he makes a coarse remark about Angel which leads her to stab Alec with a carving knife; she catches up with Angel, he shields her in country areas for a week; they are arrested at Stonehenge; Tess is tried , convicted and hanged.

HUETT, IZZ, milkmaid who works with Tess and has such a crush on Angel she tries to drown herself; she meets him again after the break-up of the marriage with Tess and confesses that she loves him 'down to the ground: did you never guess?'; Angel asks her to go to Brazil; she accepts but when she tells him that Tess would have laid down her life for him he is moved and changes his mind.

TRINGHAM, REV. MR, snobbish local parson and amateur archivist who pompously informs Jack Durbeyfield that his forbears were the noble family of D'Urberville who for centuries after the Norman Conquest held vast lands and riches; with this nonsense pumped into Durbeyfield's head he inadvertently triggers Tess's tragedy.

THE TRUMPET-MAJOR

Set against the background of threatened invasion of England by Napoleon, gentle Anne Garland is wooed by two brothers; high-minded trumpet-major John eventually stands down in favour of down to earth sailor Robert

DERRIMAN, BENJAMIN ('Uncle Benjy'), about 60, wealthy reclusive miserly landowner, fearful for his assets and frightened of his nephew Festus; entrusts tin box of his papers to Anne Garland and leaves her the bulk of his estate; dies of heart attack.

DERRIMAN, FESTUS, handsome, tall, burly red-haired yeoman soldier; braggart, drunkard, bully, coward; woos and tries to rape Anne Garland; marries Matilda Johnson.

***GARLAND, ANNE**, pretty, gentle, modest, shy, but with strong sense of honour and decency and a mind of her own; beloved of brothers John and Robert Loveday; marries Robert.

GARLAND, MRS MARTHA, aged 40, widow of landscape painter and the tenant of part of Overcombe Mill; good-natured, class-conscious, somewhat impetuous; anxious to see her only child Anne marry well; she herself marries mill owner Loveday.

GEORGE, King of England, regular and popular visitor to Budmouth, while strolling in a side street of the resort with his doctor, comes across Anne Garland weeping over the departure of Robert Loveday on HMS Victory and offers kindly words of comfort.

HARDY, Captain, accedes to Robert Loveday's application to join the crew of his command, HMS Victory, just before Battle of Trafalgar.

JOHNSON, MATILDA, *demi-mondaine* and actress, knew John Loveday before the story begins; briefly engaged to Robert Loveday; plays in theatre production in Budmouth; marries Festus Derriman.

LOVEDAY, the MILLER, aged 55 to 60, hard-working genial owner of Overcombe Mill a few miles from Budmouth; marries Mrs Martha Garland; father to John and Robert Loveday.

***LOVEDAY, JOHN,** 32, idealistic trumpet-major in a regiment of dragoons preparing to repel Napoleonic invasion; posted to Overcombe and then further afield; loves Anne Garland but stands back so she can marry brother Robert; goes to the Peninsular War never to return.

***LOVEDAY, ROBERT** ('Cap'n Bob'), 28, one-time mate of the brig Pewit *(sic);* brave capable kindly but easily fooled by women; briefly engaged to Matilda Johnson and later involved with unnamed woman; volunteers to serve in HMS Victory, sees action at Trafalgar and takes part in Nelson's funeral parade; is promoted to lieutenant; marries Anne Garland.

TWO ON A TOWER

*When a man loves a woman 10 years older, is he conqueror –
or victim?*

***CONSTANTINE, VIVIETTE LADY**, handsome late
twenties, black-haired, black-eyed, wife of landowner, has an
affectionate temperament languishing for something to do; as
overbearing baronet husband Sir Blount (away hunting lions in
Africa for two years) has barred her from taking part in social
life because he is possessive, she is described as 'neither maid,
wife or widow'; on her estate is a fine tower in Tuscan style on
top of a hill surrounded by fir plantation; idly she goes
exploring one day and finds youth Swithin St. Cleeve using the
top as observation post with his telescope; bored, she is drawn
to his personal force and charm; she orders equipment for him
to develop his tower observatory; she visits him when he
becomes ill and kisses him passionately; in love with him, she
realises the dangers when she is told her husband has died on
safari and that she is now free; Swithin tells her he loves her,
and she says their relationship now has a 'heartaching
extremity'; they marry in secret and live apart because of
servants' gossip, except for joint visits to the tower; Viviette's
brother Louis arrives from abroad, tells her she should remarry
and doubles pressure on her after he sees how the visiting
bishop is smitten with her; Louis is furious when she refuses
the bishop's proposal of marriage; from her solicitors she gets
a letter explaining that her husband died not a year ago but
only some months later – Sir Blount was still alive when she
married Swithin and that marriage is therefore invalid; she
urges Swithin to marry her again but starts to rethink, all the
more as she notes in his bustling about the tower that for him
astronomy is still tops and the rest, even marriage, well behind;
riffling through his papers she finds a letter from his solicitors
reminding him £400 per annum provided he does *not* marry is
becoming payable; he tells her why he ignored it – she reflects

she is too old for him and that 'she had led him like a child'; she tells him that he must go to the Cape; they have a last tryst at the tower; she finds she is pregnant but he has already sailed; in despair she goes to the tower where his equipment has been cleared and thinks of throwing herself down; Louis learns of her situation and pressures her and the bishop; she accepts the renewed offer of marriage as realistic solution; her boy is born and accepted as the bishop's son; the bishop dies and she goes back to her own home with the boy, fair-haired like his father; she is reminiscing at the top of the tower when Swithin is back from his travels; she realises he no longer loves her; when he says out of a sense of duty: 'Viviette I have come to marry you', she has a heart attack and dies.

GLANVILLE, LOUIS, 30, dark-eyed like his sister Viviette, worldly-wise traveller and one-time diplomat, comes to stay at the manor and presses Viviette to recover status by remarrying; seeing his sister and Swithin together he suspects a liaison which she denies, but he gets her to admit she loves the youth; she remains firm in refusing the bishop; he leaves the manor in a fury; when he learns Viviette is pregnant, as a true man of the world he knocks heads together for a quick ceremony.

HELMSDALE, DR CUTHBERT, tall, dark, unworldly bachelor bishop who conducts confirmation service is entertained to lunch by Viviette and is greatly taken by this 'warm young widow'; in an elegant letter he proposes marriage and is refused; Louis persuades him to try again and he succeeds; her baby is passed off as his son; he dies at age 50 never knowing he was duped.

LARK, TABITHA, pretty country girl, employed by Lady Constantine to read to her; occasional organist in the parish church; she is confirmed at the same service as is Swithin, who helps her when some belongings spill from her handkerchief; Viviette's brother Louis sees sexual meaning in their interaction; at this confirmation 'Swithin's more natural mate would have been one of the muslin-clad maidens who were to be presented to the bishop that day' – *a narrator's comment which seems to prefigure a relationship between Swithin and Tabitha in the future.*

*****ST. CLEEVE, SWITHIN**, 20, exceptionally 'beautiful youth' with curly fair hair; was orphaned young with income of only £80 per annum; has a passion in life to become Astronomer Royal; he uses the tower as though it is his own and enthuses the bored and lonely Viviette Constantine; the relationship deepens; soon after the news that Blount has died he hears locals gossiping that the lady of the manor can now get herself a new husband any time and that she has one lined up; Swithin at last realises how the relationship looks to a cynical world; he declares his love; they decide to marry in secret because of gossip; on the day of the wedding he gets a letter saying he has been left a legacy of £400 per annum provided he does *not* marry before he is 25 but he ignores it, marries Viviette and they go to their respective homes; resuming starwatch on the tower; at a church service he is confirmed and helps Tabitha Lark, fellow-candidate for confirmation, when she drops a thimble and purse during the service; it is seen by Viviette's brother as 'a sort of by-play going on...which means mating'; the bishop visits the tower to see the observatory and spots a coral bracelet Viviette left behind; he accuses Swithin of moral laxity and the young husband sadly asks him to suspend judgement; when Swithin's legacy comes to light he tells Viviette what he did for her sake; she tells him to go and further his work at the Cape; in the tower they spend a last evening together; in Africa he considers 'that curious pathetic chapter in his life'; back in Britain he meets Tabitha who offers to write up his scientific notes; he goes to the tower and finds Viviette there with their son; he knows he no longer loves her but with a sense of duty he says: 'Viviette, I have come to marry you!'; she dies from shock; he looks around and in the valley below, he spots Tabitha, 'a bright spot of colour'.

UNDER THE GREENWOOD TREE

*Hardy's subtitle: 'A Rural Painting of the Dutch School';
also, a tale of the 'progress' of technology.*

*****DAY, FANCY,** tall, with fine dark eyes and rich, dark
brown hair, new schoolteacher in the Mellstock hamlet; agrees
privately to marry Dick Dewy; Farmer Shinar makes a pass at
her but it repulsed; at the Harvest Thanksgiving she plays the
organ for the first time and wins the heart of Maybold the
village parson; that afternoon he comes round to ask her to
marry him and she, rather bowled over, accepts although
pledged to Dick; she gets a letter from him next day saying he
has heard the truth from Dick and wishing her luck; Fancy
happily marries Dick, drives away with him in his new cart but
will not tell of her meeting with Maybold.

DAY, GEOFFREY, gamekeeper, protective of his daughter
Fancy, not knowing of Dick's courtship he gives Farmer
Shinar permission to woo her; when Dick asks for her hand he
bluntly refuses, stressing Fancy's education and social
standing; his daughter starts refusing food and generally giving
the impression she is pining away, so Geoffrey relents.

*****DEWY, DICK,** 20, helps run his father's business and is
also a spirited fiddler in the Mellstock band; struck by new
arrival Fancy Day he dances with her at his father's Christmas
party. he transports her goods from her father's house to her
own cottage; he meets her by chance in a seaside town, she
accepts a lift in his spring-cart, and on the way home, after
much banter, he proposes and is accepted but they keep it
private; he approaches her father Mr Day but is soundly
rebuffed and he is too gentle to press his suit; tells Maybold he
is her chosen man without knowing that Fancy gave way to an
impulse; Dick becomes partner in the family firm and weds
Fancy.

DEWY, REUBEN, 40, runs a tranting business (freelance transport deliveries); leader of Mellstock choir of singers and players; genial and hospitable; he gets Maybold to delay replacing the traditional choir with the more modern organ; at changeover time, Harvest Thanksgiving, with Fancy playing the organ for the first time the choir, now denied access to the gallery where they always used to play, sit glumly with their wives in the nave.

DEWY, WILLIAM, 70, kind-hearted patriarch of the family and of the choir, good bass-viol player; adamant that it would be improper for Dewy household's Christmas dancing to begin until after midnight on Christmas Day.

MAYBOLD, ARTHUR, good-looking young man with timid mouth, is new parson demanding change; wants the traditional choir replaced by an organ; Reuben Dewy, the men's leader, goes to negotiate and it is agreed the changeover will be delayed; at Harvest Thanksgiving, Maybold is so struck by the beautiful young woman at the organ that he smartly comes around to propose marriage, promising Fancy a pony-carriage and anything else she desires; impulsively she accepts, then shocked at herself she tells him to leave; he meets Dick who reveals that he and Fancy are committed; Maybold writes to Fancy and the matter is ended.

SHINAR, FRED, local farmer and churchwarden, flies into terrific passion when woken by Mellstock carol singers at midnight on Christmas Eve; suggests to Parson Maybold the choir be replaced by an organ; he is a third suitor for Fancy but gets nowhere.

THE WELL-BELOVED

*A man with deep artistic feeling and a loving heart falls three
times for a woman of the same name.*

The hero

***PIERSTON, JOCELYN,** born on the Isle of Portland,
only son of a well-to-do stonemason, is **at 20** a 'sculptor of
budding fame' in London; he comes back to the place of his
birth after some years and meets once again childhood friend
Avice Caro who kisses him soundly; he proposes marriage;
Avice is for him an expression of the Well-Beloved he has
always sought in every woman he meets, an ideal, a spirit, a
frenzy, a 'light of the eye'; however, Jocelyn meets within
hours a well-dressed woman in furs and quickly his Well-
Beloved moves into his new friend, Marcia; he promptly
proposes marriage but when there is a delay over the licence
she cools off and another Well-Beloved image fades; he
throws himself into his work; he prospers but still keeps seeing
his ideal;

At 40, he meets Nicola Pine-Avon at a London party and
feels the Well-Beloved stir again; going back to the island he
meets Ann Avice Carow, a laundrywoman and the daughter of
Avice; this Ann Avice confesses to Jocelyn that her heart can
never stay still but moves from love to love – just like his does;
Nicola comes to the island and makes herself available but he
is too struck with Ann Avice, who he brings to London to
work for him in the hope of winning her, but she rejects as
nonsense his proposal of marriage and in any case she is
married already; resilient Jocelyn takes her back to the island
and reunites her with her husband;

At 60, he revisits the island and sees the third Avice, tall
and elegant, every bit like her grandmother but more polished;
the flame burns up again but Avice regards him as too old;
with her mother's support he arranges to marry her but just
hours beforehand she runs off with French tutor Henri Leverre,

stepson of the Marcia he had loved 40 years earlier; with Avice's departure Jocelyn reflects sadly his life has been like a ghost story; Marcia comes to see him about her stepson but stays to nurse him as his health fades; Marcia and Jocelyn marry.

The heroine(s)
*(i)*CARO, AVICE, aged 17 or 18, brown hair and bright hazel eyes, widow's only child, meets childhood friend Jocelyn on his return and kisses him hard, for which she is rebuked by her mother; she accepts him as her suitor; after Pierston leaves for London she marries her cousin Jim Caro and leaves *a daughter*…

*(ii)*CARO, ANN AVICE, brown-haired laundry girl going on 19; Jocelyn at 40 meets her in the island and brings her to London to work in his flat so he can win her love; they speak of love and she says she finds her affection flitting from one to another in quick succession. She confesses she is married already; Jocelyn gets her and her husband Isaac together in time for the birth of *a daughter*…

*(iii)*CARO, AVICE is at 20 tall, elegant, well-educated; when 61-year-old Pierston sees her 'it was very she…who had kissed him 40 years before'; he meets her on a walk and rescues her when her foot is stuck in a rock; he tells her mother he is willing to marry her; her mother supports him but for Avice he is much too old; she elopes with French admirer; the shock kills her mother.

The others
BENBOW, MARCIA, 'dignified, arresting, a very Juno', who Jocelyn feels is the new incarnation of the Beloved; he proposes and she accepts but her father takes her away on a world tour; 40 years later her stepson falls in love with a young Avice Caro; Marcia comes to the island to speak about this, nurses sick and ageing Jocelyn back to health – and marries him.

PINE-AVON, NICOLA, widow aged about 30, chestnut hair, dressed in black velvet and pearls, holds intellectual opinions, meets Jocelyn at a London reception and feels she was cruel to him so she comes to the isle and offers herself to him; he rejects her; Somers marries her.

PIERSTON, ISAAC ('Ike'), island stonemason, squat, black-bearded, married Ann Avice Caro; brought back to her from Guernsey at Jocelyn's instigation in time for birth of their daughter Avice; dies in a quarry accident.

SOMERS, ALFRED, society painter, friend and confidant of Pierston, who tells him of his quest for the Well-Beloved and confesses that once over a three-year period he was struck nine times, so Somers advises him he ought not to marry; calls his friend 'our only inspired sculptor'; comes to the island 20 years later to do seascapes, meets and marries Nicola Pine-Avon, by whom he has several daughters.

THE WOODLANDERS

Among the trees, anti-hero is desired by three women...

CHARMOND, MRS FELICE, aged late twenties, one-time actress, widow of a rich iron merchant, handsome face and impetuous nature, feels alien in the woodland village where she lives in a manor house and owns extensive groves and glades; she leaves for Italy sporting a fine hairpiece which is cut from the hair of Marty South; she comes back to find village doctor Fitzpiers is the man she met years ago and briefly fell in love with in Heidelberg; mutual desire revives, he visits her first openly and then clandestinely; Grace goes to see her and warns he will tire of her – Felice's response: 'I am his slave'; she hears Fitzpiers is overdue from a ride in the woods and rushes to Grace's home to inquire and finds rival Suke there too; Fitzpiers comes to her home bleeding after the blow from Melbury and in 'passionate bondage' nurses him – and takes him away; on the Continent, Fitzpiers admits he knows her splendid hairpiece comes from Marty – she is so angry and humiliated that they part; in Germany she is murdered by a rejected lover.

CREEDLE, ROBERT, Giles's gawky, ageing but faithful helper since boyhood, wears a soldier's jacket over his smock-frock; regards Charmond as a 'wanton woman'; helps Giles with big felling contract and after his death becomes Marty's helper.

DAMSON, SUKE, village flirt, meets Fitzpiers at Midsummer Eve frolics in the bushes and spends the night with him in a haystack; one evening Suke hears Fitzpiers is missing and rushes to Grace's home blubbering. Some time later, Fitzpiers comes back from the Continent and finds her celebrating her marriage to long-time swain, the sawyer Timothy Tangs, who gets his revenge for the fact that the child his bride is carrying is not his but that of Fitzpiers, sets a mantrap in the bushes intended to cripple him for life.

*****FITZPIERS, DR EDRED,** aged 26-28, handsome, with a charming face 'worthy of being modelled by a sculptor not over busy', medico setting up practice among the woodlanders; is soon attracted to Grace and marries her; also scores with Suke Damson; meets Mrs Charmond, who he briefly loved in Heidelberg years ago, and scores with her as well, neglecting his gentle young wife; only months after the marriage Fitzpiers meets a man in the woods at night and starts unburdening his mind not knowing it is his father-in-law, he bemoans his financial dependency and wishes he were free of Grace, at which Melbury in a fury calls him 'heartless villain' and knocks him off his horse; the bleeding Fitzpiers somehow crawls to the manor where Charmond cleans him up and nurses him; he decides he cannot go back to his wife; on the Continent he parts from Charmond and after some months writes to Grace that he is coming back; as she flees to Winterborne in distress they are brought together only at Winterborne's deathbed but Fitzpiers is kept much at arm's length, he is humbled, he abases himself ('I have been a vagabond, a brute'); Tim Tangs sets a mantrap for him in retaliation for his seduction of Suke but the only damage done is to Grace's gown, yet the scare so draws them that when he tells her of a Midlands practice where they can start life anew, she joins him; George Melbury sourly wonders what woman Fitzpiers will be making a pass at this time next year and decides that for his daughter the future is a forlorn hope.

*****MELBURY, GEORGE,** 60, tall thin figure, self-made timber merchant, the woodland village's leading businessman, is unhappy that the daughter he has expensively educated is loved by colleague Winterborne; when the clever educated Fitzpiers declares an interest he exerts strong pressure on Grace to take him; soon he is distressed at his daughter's unhappiness and protests to Mrs Charmond in vain; in the woods he meets Fitzpiers and having heard that Fitzpiers would welcome being relieved of his beloved daughter cries 'You heartless villain' and knocks him off his horse; finally comes to terms with the fact his daughter is going back to her husband but has strong doubts.

***MELBURY, GRACE**, 20, timber merchant's only child, mild-mannered, comes back from boarding school and is loved by – and promised to – Giles Winterborne, but she is cool as her horizons have changed; she is courted by 'coercive irresistible' Fitzpiers and marries him despite 'carking anxieties'; soon after the marriage she starts having regrets as he tells her how dissatisfied he is with everything and is clearly seeing Felice; Grace at first feels mild jealousy, then a feeling of abandonment; she meets Felice in a woodland glade and reproaches her, speaking boldly for once and warning her Fitzpiers will soon tire of her; on an evening when Fitzpiers is not home on time she sits worrying and she is joined by Sue and Felice, the three women joined together in 'affection, agonies of heart – all for a man who has wronged them'; her husband leaves her after being knocked down by Grace's father, and when Fitzpiers writes he is coming back she flees to Winterborne, who puts her up in his home and seeks shelter himself in a leaky hut nearby so her honour is not compromised; incessant rain brings on a deadly fever; with her love fully revived she gets his failing body into the dry and calls in for assistance the only doctor there is, Fitzpiers; Winterborne dies, she and Marty pray over his body and at his grave; a mantrap which a vengeful husband sets for Fitzpiers only succeeds in ripping Grace's gown but the scare finally tentatively bridges the gap between the couple; he promises a new life in a new practice far away, she goes off with him to the Midlands.

SOUTH, MARTY, aged 19/20, straight and slim, contours of womanhood undeveloped, but with a fine head of rich chestnut hair, sits in her cottage splicing hazel spars for use in thatching when visiting barber pays two guineas to cut off her abundant locks which he sells on to Mrs Charmond; Marty silently loves

Giles Winterborne but he is only interested in Grace; when Giles has died she comes into his hut to pray with Grace; finally she plants flowers on the grave whispering 'My own own love, you are mine and only mine, I can never forget 'ee.'

WINTERBORNE, GILES, 25, woodsman, cider-maker and Melbury's business associate; tall, blue-eyed; he loves Grace Melbury but her romance with Edred Fitzpiers overtakes events much to his unspoken sadness – though he himself is loved by Marty who helps him create new woodland as he has 'conjurer's touch' with tree-planting; when Grace flees to him because of her husband he shelters her in his cottage and sleeps nearby in a rain-drenched woodman's hut, divided from her by 'cruel propriety'; when she finds he is wild-eyed with fever she gets him indoors, undresses and nurses him regardless of convention and runs to the only doctor, her husband, who pronounces the case hopeless; Giles dies, and Marty joins Grace to pray over his body.

Part II: The Collections

Names in CAPITAL LETTERS are in the Index

A CHANGED MAN AND OTHER TALES

Hardy himself retrieved these eleven stories – which he called 'minor novels' – from various publications and courteously thanked editors for permission to reprint.

(1) A changed man
Dashing CAPTAIN JOHN MAUMBRY of the —th Hussars decides on a career change and become a curate, which his lively young wife Laura finds too much to take, the more as he takes over a slum parish where cholera breaks out; she is moved to a nearby village for safety and meets there

LIEUTENANT VANNICOCK of the —st Foot with whom she acts in a play; they decide to run away but at the start of their elopement they see how bravely the husband is succouring the needy and are moved to help; the husband sickens and dies; Laura is now free to marry, but the lieutenant, too, is a changed man, he suggests marriage in such a half-hearted way they decide by mutual consent not to proceed.

(2) The waiting supper
Childhood sweethearts NICHOLAS LONG, handsome yeoman, and CHRISTINE EVERARD, still in her teens, are forced apart because her father SQUIRE EVERARD prefers her to marry educated explorer JAMES BELLSTON; Long emigrates and comes back 15 years later; she explains she married Bellston but he had vanished without trace nine years ago; Nicholas and Christine decide to marry and the evening before the ceremony Christine prepares a candle-lit supper; a

local man arrives and says Bellston has just returned and is on his way; Nicholas comes but withdraws, the supper uneaten; but Bellston does not appear – then or ever; when the lovers are aged 53 and 50 a skeleton is found in a local river and it is presumed that Bellston slipped and fell while on his way to his wife; the lovers remain close to each other but never marry.

(3) Alicia's diary

ALICIA is the elder daughter of an amiable lethargic country clergyman and the story is told through her eyes; her younger sister, simple good-natured Caroline, meets on foreign holiday and gets engaged to a young French painter CHARLES DE LA FESTE, and he comes to meet the family; he has dark eyes and hair, a soft voice and an engaging manner; when he is introduced to Alicia and immediately it is love at first sight; they declare their love, Charles therefore says he cannot not marry Caroline and so goes abroad; the devoted Caroline does not suspect anything, but her health declines until her life is feared for and Alicia recalls Charles; to comfort the ailing Caroline, Alicia arranges for a *bogus* marriage ceremony so Alicia and Charles would not be punished if they married after Caroline has died (marriage with deceased wife's sister was then against the law); however, Caroline recovers and is vexed at the delay in being united with her husband; she goes in search for him in Venice; Alicia follows, it all comes out that it was deceit with good intentions and with dry lips Alicia tells Charles, 'you belong to her'; Charles says 'honour shall be my word, not love'; he marries Caroline but on the same day vanishes and is found drowned; Alicia is sure that it is suicide because of his mention of honour; four years later the REV THEOPHILUS HIGHAM who conducted the original sham ceremony marries Caroline for real.

(4) The grave by the handpost

SAMUEL HOLWAY, respected retired army sergeant, is so distressed by his only son's dislike of the army life which his father had recommended that he shoots himself; in accordance with custom at the time, the suicide was buried at a lonely crossroads in an unmarked grave without a coffin or religious ceremony and with a stake through his heart.

LUKE HOLWAY, the sergeant's son, comes from his first overseas tour of duty with a changed attitude, now loves army life and is shocked at his father's end; he arranges with sexton Ezra Cattstock to have the body reburied, pays for a headstone and leaves for the Peninsular War; comes back after Waterloo years later as a sergeant-major rich in glory, and finds his father's good name has not been restored because Cattstock had trouble in removing the stake from the heart and simply hid the headstone Luke had paid for; Luke feels humiliated and shoots himself at the crossroads; asks he be buried with his father, but the note he leaves is swept away and he is buried in the churchyard.

(5) Enter a dragoon

JOHN CLARK, corporal of the —th Dragoons, called away to serve in the Crimea War on the eve of his wedding to West Country girl Selina Paddock, leaving her with a son; he comes back as a sergeant-major, is posted in Yorkshire where he marries another woman and also has a son; this marriage breaks up; he comes to the West Country after three years to marry his first love Selina (bigamously?) and arrives to claim her on the very evening of a pre-wedding party to celebrate her coming marriage to her new man Bartholomew Miller; Clark dances with her but she does not tell him what the party is for until they have danced so long and so vigorously that he has to sit down; he suddenly becomes ill and dies of heart failure.

BARTHOLOMEW MILLER, prosperous master-wheelwright, aged about 30 and rubicund, is contented to take Selina with her boy.

SELINA PADDOCK is engaged to be married to corporal John Clark who is called away to the Crimean War just before the ceremony; she hears nothing for three years, believes he is dead and engages herself to Miller; the dragoon enters the cottage on the very evening of a party to celebrate the new union; Clark has a fatal heart attack; after the funeral she withdraws to another town and sets up in business; Miller having tactfully withdrawn comes after 18 months and asks her to marry him; she refuses preferring to carry on her business and visit Clark's grave with her son; some time later she visits the grave again and sees a woman in widow's weeds, who reveals herself as the wife who Clark left in Yorkshire and so, as she puts it, she is the *real* Mrs John Clark...

(6) A tryst at an ancient earthwork
The narrator walks up an ancient earthwork on a remote Wessex hill to meet a well-known and recognised antiquary of about 60 anxious to explore this lonely place at night in bad weather so he will not be disturbed by authority; they find a Roman mosaic pavement, then a skeleton, a fine five-inch statuette of Mercury and other items; after he is satisfied the antiquary puts everything back scrupulously, but the narrator wonders whether the Mercury was put back, too; seven years later the man is dead and a statuette is found among his effects and bequeathed to a museum.

(7) What the shepherd saw: a tale of four moonlight nights
BILL MILLS, a young shepherd watching over his ewes in his lonely hut near to a Druid trilithon by moonlight during Christmas week, sees a married woman meet an innocent admirer of long time ago but they do not realise they are secretly observed by the woman's husband, a duke and local landowner; on the second night the man appears to keep a tryst and the shepherd sees him knocked down by the duke and dragged away; on the third night the duke brings his wife to pretend to await or seek the man, of course without success and the duchess goes home; the duke discovers the shepherd has seen too much and makes him swear on the Druid monument never to reveal the secret in return for which the boy will get a new life and education; some 22 years later the boy has grown up to be the duke's unhappy steward; on yet another moonlit Christmas night, feeling restless, he returns to

the trilithon, and sees the duke in his nightshirt guiltily trying to dig something up; Mills realises the old nobleman is sleepwalking; the next morning the duke is found dead and in due time Mills himself dies and the secret never comes out, but local history has it that on moonlit Christmas nights human shapes are seen flitting by the stones, there is the gleam of a weapon and the shadow of a man dragging a burden away.

(8) A committee-man of 'The Terror'

MADEMOISELLE V—, a young French tutor staying at an English resort during the 1802 peace between England and France, meets there a strange foreigner she recognises with horror as a member of the Committee of Public Safety who sent members of her family to their deaths during The Terror; he seems down on his luck and appeals to her for help; she does so despite her revulsion and they become closer; marriage beckons despite her great misgivings; the big day approaches and she has scruples but decides to go through with it; he has scruples, too, and pulls out; Mademoiselle V— never marries.

(9) Master John Horseleigh, Knight

In the 1530s landowner SIR JOHN HORSELEIGH marries an heiress and has three children by her, then discovers she unwittingly has a husband she thought lost in the wars but survived and is living abroad; wanting legitimate issue Sir John clandestinely marries Edith Stocker, shipowner's widow, and has a daughter by her; Edith's sailor brother comes home after long absence and dislikes the way his sister is stuck out of the way with only occasional visits (as she tells him) from her husband; fearing she has been dishonoured he confronts the husband and stabs him; Sir John before he dies tells that he did what he did to avoid upset; it is a local tradition that shortly afterwards the first husband of the heiress came back to marry her for appearance's sake.

(10) The Duke's reappearance – a family tradition
Generous-spirited villager CHRISTOPHER SWETMAN gives
shelter, food and a change of clothes to a tall dark stranger
dressed like a cavalryman who comes to his door at a time of
conflict and strife in the west; the stranger refuses to give his
name and when he leaves asks his host to look after some of
his belongings, including a sword which he says belonged to
his grandfather; after he goes Swetman examines the sword, a
magnificent piece of work with pictures on the blade of King
Charles I and Queen Henrietta Maria; some time after,
following further reports of conflict, Swetman lies awake one
night and sees the stranger silently come back and retrieve his
belongings; then there are reports from London that a high-
born rebel had been executed, followed by reports that
someone one else had taken his place and that the rebel had got
away; from then on Christopher Swetman and his family
believed to the end of their days, as did many others in that
part of the country, that the visitor had been the Duke of
Monmouth.

(11) A mere interlude
DAVID HADDEGAN, prosperous businessman of about 55,
delighted to marry the calm young girl Baptista he knew when
a child; even more delighted when she confesses to him that
she has a secret and therefore he can admit he has a secret as
well – that he really wanted to marry a schoolteacher so she
could educate his stepchildren.

CHARLES STOW, schoolmaster, impetuously persuades
former flame Baptista – when she is on her way to marry a
man she does not love – to marry him instead; the day after the
ceremony he goes swimming and drowns.

BAPTISTA TREWTHEN, resigns from a school teaching job
she detests to go and marry a man who has long wanted her
and whom she does not love; on the way she meets one-time
admirer Charles Stow, who persuades her this is all wrong and
that she should marry him instead; the day afterwards he goes

swimming and drowns; she goes to her elderly fiancé David Haddegan and finds the pressure of wedding preparations and general merriment so much she feels she must keep her cool and that she must go through the second marriage; a blackmailer appears and when she realises the truth will have to come out she tells her husband about her previous marriage, rather than being shocked he professes delight, because now he need no longer conceal that he married her largely so she could act as teacher to the four stepdaughters he had from *his* previous marriage; Baptista feels trapped in teaching once again but learns to like the girls; her life enters a serene period.

A GROUP OF NOBLE DAMES

Members of a men's club in rural Wessex kept indoors by rain pass the time telling stories with the theme of fine ladies in days gone by.

(1) The First Countess of Wessex

BETTY DORRELL, married at 13 to a man of 30 by her ambitious land-owning mother; the couple are kept apart for some years but when the time draws near she deliberately has herself infected with smallpox to frighten off her husband Stephen; she elopes with a youth she has met in the meantime but he is the one who is frightened off by the marks on her face and it is Stephen who fearlessly salutes her with a kiss; the smallpox attack is light; after yet more delay she overcomes repugnance of her patient courtly husband, he is ennobled; they have many children and she is the local grande dame.

SUSAN DORRELL, owner of the largest estate for miles around, marries off her only child Betty to a man she regards as having a brilliant future; first urges delay in bringing couple together, then ironically finds that after she had herself counselled further delay the wife and husband have forestalled her and a child is expected.

THOMAS DORRELL, father of Betty on whom he dotes; he is a good-natured squire, a three-bottle man bitterly but vainly opposed to his wife's ambitious move for their child; when the husband is likely to come to claim Betty after the agreed delay of some years the squire travels to Bristol to fend him off; the trip destroys his health; just before he dies he is overjoyed to hear his darling daughter has eloped with Phelpson.

CHARLEY PHELPSON, in his teens, falls in love with Betty Dorrell; he is the 'local petty gentleman' her father originally wanted for her; he boldly carries her off from her chamber on his horse but when he sees she has smallpox it is as much as he can do to take her straight back home.

STEPHEN REYNARD, much travelled courtier and diplomatist, sagacious and gentle-mannered, aged 30 when he is wedded to schoolgirl Betty with mutual agreement to wait; when at last they meet and he sees she has smallpox he kisses her; he is made a peer, they have lots of children.

TUPCOMBE, Squire Dorrell's loyal manservant.

(2) Barbara of the House of Grebe
BARBARA GREBE, 17, heiress to a grand estate, is the marital target of neighbouring landowner Earl of Uplandtowers, but elopes to London with handsome villager Edmund Willowes; her parents send Edmund on a study tour; when he returns to Barbara after 17 month she is repelled by horrifying scars he has suffered in an accident in Venice; he goes away and when he does not return she marries the earl, who is soon incensed by her withdrawn attitude; a fine statue of himself which Willowes had made in Italy before the accident arrives and is locked away in her boudoir where she visits it regularly; her husband finds her embracing and kissing it; he has it mutilated and forces her to look at it until she feels driven to accept him fully as her husband, after giving birth 11 times in nine years she dies exhausted.

SIR JOHN GREBE, wealthy baronet, and his wife, intensely ambitious for their only child to marry the next door noble, Lord Uplandtowers.

UPLANDTOWERS, the fifth earl, at 19 already has a stern unforgiving nature; he sets out to win the hand of Barbara Grebe and dances with her twice at a Christmas party, and learns next day she has eloped with lover Willowes that very night; his reaction: 'Damn her for a fool!!'; some years pass: when he is nearing 30 and Barbara is on her own again, he marries her but is soon exasperated by her coolness; discovers her with the magnificent statue; he does some research and has it mutilated exactly the way Willowes was (nose and ears gone, hardly any lips, one eye lost); he positions it in her bedroom with backlighting to enhance the effect and forces her to look at it until her spirit is crushed.

EDMOND WILLOWES, dark-eyed and exceptionally handsome ('your Adonis, your matchless man!'), glass-painter's son, elopes with Barbara Grebe; her parents send him abroad to make him a gentleman; in Pisa a sculptor makes a statue of him; in Venice he acquits himself bravely by rescuing people in a theatre fire but is so dreadfully scarred he is forced to wear a mask; on his return to England, Barbara cannot cope and he vanishes, never to return.

(3) The Marchioness of Stonehenge
LADY CAROLINE, a young woman of rare charms, takes up with a land steward's son on her father's estate, marries him secretly; he dies suddenly of a heart attack and to cover her tracks she sets up a local girl, Milly, who had loved the young man fondly, as his widow with an adequate allowance; a child is born and Milly again fills the breach, bringing up the boy, who becomes a successful soldier and dearly loves the woman he thinks is his real mother; Caroline meanwhile has married the elderly Marquis of Stonehenge; the marquis dies and Caroline, now lonely, wishes to take the soldier back; he refuses, saying that as she was once ashamed of his father, now he is ashamed of her.

(4) Lady Mottisfont
PHILIPPA OKEHALL, placid and submissive, becomes wife of distinguished baronet Sir Ashley Mottisfont and readily agrees to take in his love-child Dorothy and bring her up, becoming passionately fond of her; the child's natural mother, now a wealthy widowed Contessa, becomes a neighbour and also wants her; after a battle of emotions the child herself decides in favour of the Contessa; when the Contessa marries again Dorothy is really in the way and Sir Ashley and Philippa

are urged to take her back but Philippa now has a son of her own and refuses; after all, Dorothy once made her own choice; the doubly-rejected Dorothy is farmed out to a cottage family and eventually marries well; Philippa remains happy with her son.

5) The Lady Icenway
MARIA HEYMERE, 19, with great beauty and imperious temper, marries and goes abroad to South America with a rich Dutchman; when he confesses he is already married she goes back to England and sets herself up as a widow with the child of the marriage; she marries the huntin' shootin' peer Lord Icenway; her original husband breaks his promise and contacts her, later returning to beg only to be allowed to see his son, she agrees; he gets himself a job as Lord Icenway's gardener to be nearby; when he dies, Lady Icenway puts up in the local church a memorial window 'erected by his grieving widow'.

(6) Squire Petrick's Lady
SQUIRE PETRICK is told by his dying wife that he is not the father of the son just born to her; he alters his will to cut the boy out; he learns that the biological father is heir to a dukedom, which so fills him with pride he illicitly alters the succession back again; he meets a doctor who tells him that the squire's lady had great imaginings and that anyway the young nobleman could not possibly have been involved so the child is really his; disappointed, he resents the boy.

(7) Anna, Lady Baxby
LADY BAXBY is about to leave her husband's castle to meet her soldier brother (at the time of the Civil War) when she hears on the outskirts a young woman's voice complaining that she was 'afeared' my lord 'would never come'; she turns back immediately to the marital bedroom and ties a piece of string from a bedpost to her husband's hair; he sleeps through the night and it turns out it was a casual assignation he had quite forgotten.

(8) The Lady Penelope

LADY PENELOPE, a beautiful, brave and buxom damsel, has three ardent suitors and in a light-hearted moment she says: 'In faith, I will marry you all in turn'; the first one she marries dies 'of his convivialities' after a few months; the second, who turns out to be a bully, also dies; the third hears talk of suspicious circumstances after all these deaths and leaves, discomfited; Penelope sickens and he comes back to her in time for her to deny wrongdoing; she dies and he realises she was 'done to death by a vile scandal that was wholly unfounded'.

(9) The Duchess of Hamptonshire

EMMELINE OLDBOURNE, with a sweet and simple nature, daughter of a snobbish rector, loves his young curate but is married off to the rough and brutal Duke of Hamptonshire; the youth visits her secretly and says he is emigrating; she begs to come with him but he says that is 'forbidden in God's law'; the only interruption in the tedium of his long sea journey to America is that he is asked to conduct the funeral service for a steerage passenger; in 10 years in the U.S. he prospers; reading in a newspaper of the duke's death he sails back hoping to claim his lost love; in England he learns that she ran away 10 years ago and, sailing for America in steerage, fell ill and was buried at sea.

(10) The Honourable Laura

LAURA NORTHBROOK, young, newly married and impetuous, elopes with an opera singer; her husband finds her; the singer tries to murder him but he survives and is tended very lovingly by Laura in the hope he will forgive her but he doesn't, saying: 'I don't like you'; she is left sad and lonely; after 12 years (she is now 29) the husband comes back and forgives her; a son is born.

LIFE'S LITTLE IRONIES

(1) An Imaginative Woman

WILL MARCHMILL, tall, brown beard, down to earth, is a successful arms manufacturer with his soul in his work; the mother of his three children is ELLA MARCHMILL, 30, slim, elegant, pretty, with sparkling dark eyes, who has become emotionally isolated and sought refuge in a world of her own, publishing some poems under the nom-de-plume John Ivy; on a summer holiday in a coastal resort they hire quarters recently occupied by a shy and romantic poet Robert Trewe who has published successfully; Ella feels increasingly drawn to this man who echoes her own feelings and needs, the more as she finds some scribbles of his verse on the wall above her bed; she hopes that in this small town their paths may cross but somehow it never happens; they exchange notes and he replies courteously to Mr John Ivy; when the holiday ends the Marchmills go back home and Ella reads in the paper that the poet shot himself as he was depressed because he never met a woman really devoted to him; the effect on her is devastating as she feels she could have filled such a role to their mutual enrichment; she goes into decline and dies giving birth to her fourth child, her last words to her husband being 'I wanted a fuller appreciator... rather than another lover'; some years later Marchmill chances upon the poet's photograph and a lock of his hair, takes a close look at his youngest son and sees there, by a trick of nature, strong traces of resemblance; in his matter-of-fact way he believes the worst and though Ella was completely innocent he angrily rejects the child.

(2) The son's veto.

SOPHY is a good-natured simple country girl, a child of nature, parlour-maid to MR TWYCOTT, a wealthy vicar; she is wooed by SAM HOBSON, a young gardener, but she refuses him in favour of Mr Twycott who is lonely and who has lost his first wife; the couple move to London where he dies, leaving Sophy Twycott to look after their son RANDOLPH, who goes to a public school and moves in a very different milieu; Sophy is bored and lonely, all the more as an accident has confined her to a wheelchair; she chances again upon Sam, now in the vegetable trade; without Randolph's knowledge she accepts rides on his produce cart to Covent Garden, a great thrill in her drab existence; Sam proposes marriage again; after long and painful hesitation she broaches the subject to her son and gradually reveals Sam's status; Randolph first bursts into tears, then says such a step would 'degrade me in the eyes of all the gentlemen of England', and finally makes her swear not to marry without his consent; Randolph studies at Oxford but always remains adamant; when Sophy dies, on the way to her funeral a young smooth-shaven priest in the mourning-carriage scowls at the greengrocer who respectfully doffs his cap as the hearse passes.

(3) For Conscience' Sake

After fretting for 20 years because he promised to marry a girl in the West Country and abandoned her and her child, lonely London bachelor MILLBORNE resolves to mend matters and seeks them out; he finds the woman and her daughter well settled and respected as dance and music teachers; he tells MRS LEONORA FRANKLAND he wishes to make retribution and is initially rebuffed as causing needless upset; he overcomes her scruples, they marry, and the couple and daughter FRANCES move to London, where they are visited by the girl's suitor, the REV. PERCIVAL COPE; Cope shrewdly spots resemblance between Frances and her new stepfather and drawing his conclusions pulls out; mother and daughter bitterly upbraid Millborne, the mother particularly for ruining her life twice; the much-embarrassed Millborne settles the women in a house in the west with ample income while he retires to Brussels, where he seeks solace in alcohol for his exaggerated sense of moral duty, and learns with momentary satisfaction that Frances marries her man.

(4) A Tragedy of Two Ambitions

Hard-up brothers JOSHUA and CORNELIUS HALBOROUGH struggle to get away from the influence of their drunken wastrel father, work fantastically hard and despite all obstacles achieve their aim to become clergymen; they also manage to have their pretty sister Rosa expensively educated; Joshua becomes curate to a wealthy country family where the squire wants to marry Rosa; their father comes up at a crucial moment, having just been released from prison, and drunkenly reveals that Joshua was born before his parents were married, and that he is out to meet the squire; the brothers are appalled at the danger to them all; they hear him tumble into a stream; steel-willed Joshua holds his more gentle brother back and they let their father drown; they retrieve and hide his walking stick cut from living wood; an unknown and unrecognisable body is washed up at the weir and buried, Joshua officiating at the funeral; Rosa marries her squire, a son is born, but the brothers remain troubled; they go back to the weir and retrieve the walking stick, finding it has sprouted new life – a stem of silver-poplar; quietly they confirm to each other that they, too, would have liked to have 'put an end to trouble here in this self-same spot'.

(5) On the Western Circuit

Junior barrister CHARLES BRADFORD RAYE from Lincoln's Inn chances to meet simple country girl Anna riding on a roundabout at a country fair; they are drawn to each other; when he has to go on circuit he writes to her asking for a letter back; as Anna, a maidservant, cannot read or write she pleads with her sympathetic employer EDITH HARNHAM to write for her but things get out of hand when a regular correspondence develops; Edith, unhappily married and lonely, expresses increasingly her own emotions rather than Anna's; when Anna reveals she is pregnant Edith has to take over completely, and as Anna cannot cope, arranges a wedding in London to which she has to go as well; immediately after the ceremony it becomes painfully clear that Anna is a child of nature – and that Edith did the letters; Raye tells Edith: 'Legally I have married her... but in soul and in spirit I have married you and no other woman'; they kiss and part for good; Raye goes on his honeymoon and in the train his wife asks what he is doing and he replies sadly: 'Reading over all those sweet letters signed "Anna"'.

(6) To Please His Wife

Level-headed decent young sailor SHADRACH JOLLIFFE comes back to his home port from surviving shipwreck on the Newfoundland banks and gets involved with two young women, shy delicate EMILY HANNING and bold large-framed JOANNA PHIPPARD; he is drawn more towards Emily, and a tender understanding develops; Joanna is much bolder and draws Jolliffe away from her friend out of envy; Jolliffe comes to realise Emily is really for him but he feels duty-bound to fulfil his engagement with Joanna, and they marry; he forsakes the sea and they set up a grocer's which never prospers while the gentle Emily marries a wealthy merchant, Joanna feeling acutely the difference how their fortunes have changed; Jolliffe decides to go to sea again and comes back with some £300, not really enough, so Joanna pressures him to go to sea again and even agrees to let their sons George and Jim go as well to maximise profits, so making them 'the slaves of her ambition'; the ship does not return; six years go by and Joanna becomes grey and frail; one night she fancies hearing the footsteps of her husband and sons, runs into the street barefoot and knocks at the grocery door; the new occupant tells her: 'No, nobody has come'.

(7) The Fiddler of the Reels

WAT OLLAMOOR, fiddler, dandy and company-man, commonly known as Mop because of his thick head of curly and unruly hair, is a gifted extempore violinist always exciting with his jigs and reels the passions of village girls; in the case of young CAR'LINE ASPENT so much so that she rejects the advances of respectable mechanic NED HIPCROFT; disgruntled Ned heads for London to work; four years later he gets a letter from Car'line saying she has been foolish and would like to marry him after all; she arrives in London – with a little daughter; Ned agrees to take them both; some time later they feel the need to return to the country; while Ned goes job-hunting she and the child Carry go into a wayside inn where she sees Mop again entrancing the customers; Car'line is induced to dance and he deliberately increases the tempo of the reels so that at last she is left dancing convulsively alone and then collapses; Ned arrives in time to help revive her – but Mop and the child are gone; they are never seen again: it is surmised they went to America where he taught his daughter to dance so he could live off her earnings.

(8) A Few Crusted Characters
Travellers on a country coach tell each other stories

(a) Tony Kyles, the Arch-Deceiver
Commèdia rusticana: TONY KYLES, lusty young carter struggles (in vain) to keep apart three pretty girls all in his vehicle at the same time and all engaged to him.

(b) The History of the Hardcomes
Cousins STEVE HARDCOME and JAMES HARDCOME decide to swap fiancées just before their weddings; the original couples are ultimately reunited, one in life, the other in death.

(c) The Superstitious Man's Story
A ghost story: on the very hour that he died WILLIAM PRIVETT is seen at the spot where his only son drowned years ago.

(d) Andrey Satchel and the Parson and Clerk
ANDREY SATCHEL arrives for his wedding drunk with his heavily pregnant bride; the parson agrees to lock the couple in the church until the groom sobers up but he himself is so carried away by the excitement of the local hunt he doesn't go back to them until the next morning; he then marries them and

lets the newlyweds come to the rectory and 'eat till they could hold no more'.

(e) Old Andrey's Experience as a Musician
Andrey's father, also ANDREY SATCHEL, in his totally unmusical youth, wanted badly to take part in the local Christmas concert of the local choir (i.e., band) at the squire's place because of the jolly supper that is to follow, but he is sadly exposed (and expelled) when he holds his borrowed violin clumsily and upside down; he still gets his feed in the servants' hall, though.

(f) Absent-Mindedness in a Parish choir
To keep warm on a bitterly cold night the parish choir (band) led by NICHOLAS PUDDINGCOME enjoy a noggin or three of hot brandy and beer, and nod off during the evening service; nudged awake, they start immediately their favourite jig; the scandalised squire replaces them with a barrel-organ that plays 22 good hymns – and no jigs.

(g) The Winters and the Palmleys
Honest simple JACK WINTER so completely bungles his attempt to steal back some love-letters from a former love that he ends up on the gallows.

(h) Incident in the Life of Mr George Crookhill
Cross and double-cross on the high road? Con artist GEORGE CROOKHILL finds a victim who look very promising – and unexpectedly finds himself on the *right* side of the law.

(i) Netty Sargent's copyhold
Quick-witted NETTY SARGENT positions the corpse of her newly-dead uncle in such a way that it looks as if he is renewing the lease on their cottage; the land agent is taken in, and she and her husband have a home.

WESSEX TALES

(1) The Three Strangers

While a storm rages outside on the heath, in their lonely cottage the hospitable shepherd Fennel and his wife host a merry party to celebrate the christening of their new daughter; the festivities are interrupted by the arrival, one by one, of three men who are not what they seem.

(2) A Tradition of Eighteen Hundred and Four

A retired shepherd sits in a chimney corner and relates that around the year 1804 when an invasion from France seemed imminent, he as a young lad was out guarding sheep near Lulworth Cove on a moonlit night, accompanied by his uncle, when he saw two men in cocked hats conversing, not in English but apparently in French, one with a chart in his hand, consulting with another, to whom he was very deferential; both gestured towards the lie of the land; light falls on the senior man's face and the uncle says he recognises him from pictures; the two men go down to the cove and are rowed to a waiting vessel; it was never confirmed but in those parts to this day the tradition is that discussing a possible landing site for an invasion were a French general and his commander NAPOLEON.

(3) The Melancholy Hussar of the German Legion

In the reign of George III, MATTHÄUS TINA, 22, a Hussar of the King's German Legion stationed near Weymouth, depressed and gloomy at being in a foreign country far from his old mother in Saarbruck *(sic),* is befriended by shy local girl PHYLLIS GROVE, already engaged to an absentee fiancé; they decide to elope to Germany, but the fiancé comes back, she tells her Hussar therefore she cannot go through with it; however, her fiancé has actually come to tell her he has married someone else; sadly she feels it is too late to call back

Matthāus who has already left camp; from her cottage overlooking the camp a few days later she watches horror-stricken as her Hussar is paraded in front of the entire regiment and shot for desertion.

(4) The Withered Arm

Fresh-faced newlywed GERTRUDE LODGE, 19, arrives at the dairy farm of her well-to-do husband; her arrival arouses bitterness in RHODA BROOK, a haggard milkmaid of 30 employed on the farm, who lives with the son she bore Gertrude's husband some 12 years ago and who was then cast off; her misgivings run so deep that one night she dreams of the new bride coming towards her threateningly and Rhoda grabbing her by the left arm and violently thrusting her away; the two women eventually meet and Rhoda is won over by Gertrude's sweet manner; they become friendly and one day the younger woman shows Rhoda a discoloration on her arm; Rhoda is shocked at seeing it has the outline of her own fingers, all the more when she learns the trouble began the night of the dream; she reflects later that local people have held her to possess black magic powers since she had a child out of wedlock; later that summer the women meet and Gertrude shows her the skin on the arm has gone grey; they meet again, the arm is worse, Rhoda names for a possible cure a rural hermit/soothsayer Conjuror Trendle, who tells her an enemy did this to her; word gets around that the harm was caused by Gertrude Lodge being 'over-looked' by Rhoda Brook; mother and her son quit the area; six years go by, Gertrude's arm is worse and her husband has withdrawn from her because of it; desperate and haggard herself, she visits Trendle again; he says there is but one chance – to touch with your arm the neck of a man newly hanged, 'after he is cut down but the body is still warm' because this will 'turn her blood'; patiently over months she checks with the county jail and in July finds a hanging planned; her husband being conveniently away, she goes to the town and bribes the hangman; just after the execution she is admitted to a cell where the body lies; the hangman lays her arm against a thin red line on the dead man's neck, she shrieks; at the same moment another door opens and in come Rhoda Brook and her husband, who have come to collect the body of their executed son; Gertrude, her blood indeed 'turned', dies three days later.

(5) Fellow-Townsmen

GEORGE BARNET, town councillor, has long loved naval officer's modest daughter LUCY SAVILE but for status and influence marries a tall haughty woman who feels she could have done better than to marry just a prominent citizen of a small town, so she treats him contemptuously and eventually walks out; when he later gets news she has died he feels he is at last free to marry his Lucy, only to hear that on that very day she is to marry a fellow-townsman to whom he had introduced her; disappointed, he quits, travels for 21 years and when he returns hears that Lucy is now a widow; immediately, he meets her and proposes; she thanks him politely but says she has no intention of remarrying, then thinks it over and goes after him, but finds he has left town – and does not return.

(6) Interlopers at The Knap

In a remote country house called The Knap, comely independent-minded SALLY HALL and her mother are preparing a festive spread for the arrival of farmer CHARLES DARTON, 32 with a large-scale farm (turnover £30,000 per annum), who is going to take her away as his wife; the preparations are interrupted by the arrival of a thin figure, destitute, gravely ill and in rags: it is Sally's brother Philip, who set out to make a new life in Australia years ago and made a hash of it; with him are his wife Helen and two small children; Sally and her mother help them where they can, and when Farmer Darton arrives and meets the family Sally notices an immediate interaction between Darton and Helen; cool-headed Sally senses that she is not going to marry Darton; later that evening Philip dies in the room upstairs; it transpires that Helen and Darton had a relationship before she decided to go to Australia; the wedding between Sally and Darton is postponed and Darton goes home with the elder orphaned child to take care of; Sally having learned about the background from Helen suggests to Darton he marries Helen instead; he does so but when the fragile Helen dies in childbirth; he feels he is now free to try again with Sally, always the better choice; exactly five years later, she refuses him; months and years go by, he tries again but Sally turns down both him and several other suitable men.

(7) The Distracted Preacher

RICHARD STOCKDALE, modest grocer's son, is sent to Dorset to minister to local nonconformists; he is tall, curly-haired, kind, earnest; he finds lodgings with young widow LIZZY NEWBERRY; on his first night he has a cold which she cures with rum from a smuggled barrel, and she explains the village has been in the local industry of landing French liquor for years; he is intrigued by her and puzzled by her irregular hours when she is apparently away all night; she is so lively and distracts him so much from his job of writing sermons that he asks her to marry him; he urges her to give up this 'blamable and dangerous practice' but the next night is induced to accompany her to Lulworth Cove; he sees her capably land a consignment; the smugglers win in a clash with Customs officers; Lizzy says smuggling is in her blood and as both refuse to change their ways he leaves the village; two years later he looks her up, finds the smuggling racket has been smashed; he takes her to his new place and she becomes the good minister's wife.

A Quiz on Who's Who in Thomas Hardy

1.   What did Tess call her child?

2.   Who did Marty South love in vain?

3.   Who shot Sergeant Troy?

4.   Who were really star-struck lovers?

5.   A rum plot for a man of God to be involved in?

6.   Why was Diggory's face red?

7.   An illustrious visitor to Lulworth Cove, perhaps?

8.   What happened to Father Time?

9.   What did young Michael Henchard do at the country fair?

10.   Which sculptor fell in love three times?

11.   Who was compelled to view her lover's mutilated statue?

12.   Nice work if you can get it: £100,000 contract to redo a castle?

13.   Who rescued her suitor from a clifftop by making a rope of her underwear?

14.   A violinist of genius who has a way with the girls?

And there's a crib overleaf

Answers to the quiz:

1. What did Tess call her child?
   Sorrow. *Tess of the D'Urbervilles*

2. Who did Marty South love in vain?
   Winterborne. *The Woodlanders*

3. Who shot Sergeant Troy?
   Boldwood. *Far from the Madding Crowd*

4. Who were really star-struck lovers?
   Swithin and Viviette. *Two on a Tower*

5. A rum plot for a man of God to be involved in?
   Smuggling. *The Distracted Preacher, Wessex Tales*

6. Why was Diggory's face red?
   He peddled red dye to sheep farmers. *The Return of the Native*

7. An illustrious visitor to Lulworth Cove. Perhaps Napoleon? *A Tradition of Eighteen Hundred and Four. Wessex Tales*

8. What happened to Father Time?
   Hanged himself. *Jude the Obscure*

9. What did young Michael Henchard do at the country fair?
   Sold his wife. *The Mayor of Casterbridge*

10. Which sculptor fell in love three times
    Jocelyn Pierston. *The Well-Beloved*

11.   Who was compelled to view her lover's mutilated statue?
      Barbara Grebe. *A Group of Noble Dames*

12.   Nice work if you can get it: £100,000 contract to redo a castle?
      Paula Power's Stancy Castle. *A Laodicean*

13.   Who rescued her suitor from a clifftop by making a rope of her underwear?
      Elfride. *A Pair of Blue Eyes*

14.   A violinist of genius who has a way with the girls?
      Wat Ollamoor (Mop). *Fiddler of the reels*